About

Dispelling Myths and Clari, ...g ... ...ical Message of God's Overflowing Grace

Eddie Snipes

A book by:
Exchanged Life Discipleship

MW01145290

Published by GES Book Publishing
Carrollton, GA

Copyright © 2013 by Eddie Snipes, Exchanged Life Discipleship, and GES Book Publishing

http://www.exchangedlife.com

ISBN: 978-0615956558

Contact the author by visiting http://www.eddiesnipes.com or
http://www.exchangedlife.com

Table of Contents

The Purpose of This Book

If you truly want to know what grace teaching is all about, this book will explain many of the major teachings of grace. I'm confident that the following chapters will persuade you that grace is the gospel. If you honestly read this book with a desire to know the truth of what the Bible teaches about grace, you'll be driven to the inevitable conclusion that the gospel is about the finished work of Christ given to us, and not the works based belief system that we must do for God.

Many oppose the gospel of grace because it empowers the believer to be receivers of God and not dependent upon teachers. Each one of us are called the anointed because we are in Christ. Each person has the promise, "You don't need any man to teach you." You have been given victory and you are already an overcomer.

The following chapters will explain the victory of the believer based on receiving God's promises by faith while also dispelling the misconceptions about grace that cause people to distrust the gospel.

Creating fear is how people are kept in bondage and under control. We are called to step outside of fear and have confidence in Christ, the head of the church and our Good Shepherd. Those who teach that any part of the way of faith is a threat are using fear to usurp authority from the believer and bring attention to themselves. Any who set themselves up as lords over the flock are outside true of Christianity.

A new challenge against faith has arisen in the church. It's not a new doctrine or new secular assault against the church. It is a movement that seeks to turn Christians against fellow Christians because those who believe in faith alone are being called a threat to Christianity. It's now being called 'heresy' to believe God's promises without wavering. Books are being released as the answer to what some are calling "The greatest threat to the church in modern history."

This book is the response to those who are calling for Christians to turn on each other in the name of defending the faith. The Bible says, "Are you not carnal (or fleshly minded) when there are envy, strife, and divisions among you?"[1] Ironically those who believe in the Bible's promise of grace are being called divisive, even though the battle cry is coming from those who have a limited view of grace.

This book will dispel the misrepresentation of grace while also looking at the reality of grace as taught in scripture. The goal of this publication is to persuade you not to allow others to poison your mind against true faith in Christ. Martin Luther stood upon faith alone and was called a heretic. Now modern churchianity is falling into the same mindset that had no tolerance of grace by faith in the 1500s. The myths of hyper-grace will be clearly dispelled. Even more importantly, the truth of scripture will be the litmus test for what is true and why we believe as we do. It is the Bible that uses terms like exceedingly and abundantly to describe grace.

It's vital for you to understand the depth of grace, for until we understand the promise that we have been given all things through Christ, you will remain stuck in the fruitless circle of human effort and empty religion.

Since the beginning of the church, there have always been naysayers against the way of faith. The Bible warns that the man or woman of faith will be called evil.[2] Jesus warned that many would persecute His disciples while thinking they are doing God a service.[3] The Bible even forewarns those who walk by faith that their faith will be counted as evidence of wickedness to the religious establishment, but it is actually the proof of your faith in Christ. Consider the words of **Philippians 1:27-29**

> [27] Only let your conduct be worthy of the gospel of Christ, so that whether I come and see you or am absent, I may hear of your affairs, that you stand fast in one spirit, with one mind striving together for the faith of the gospel,

---

[1] 1 Corinthians 3:3
[2] Matthew 5:11
[3] John 16:2

28 and not in any way terrified by your adversaries, which is to them a proof of perdition, but to you of salvation, and that from God.

29 For to you it has been granted on behalf of Christ, not only to believe in Him, but also to suffer for His sake,

The word 'perdition' is the Greek word 'apoleia', which means utter destruction or someone perishing in eternal misery. This passage is telling us that those who will not waver from faith in Christ will be accused of being eternally lost by those who don't understand true faith.

This has been true in every era of Christian history, and it is equally true today. Jesus said, "Woe when all men speak well of you." He then goes on to say that they will curse you, speak evil of you, and persecute you. Our response should be to bless and not curse, return good for evil, and love those who express hatred.[4]

In every generation, people have risen up to establish a well-intentioned, but human standard of religion. Then any who do not adhere to the belief of the establishment are considered heretics by those who demand conformity. This is in spite of the history of religion claiming to be fighting for God while committing atrocities in the name of God. Each generation believes that their persecution of others is defending the faith, yet God never permits His people to become the persecutors.

Once someone is labeled as a heretic, the church feels justified in persecuting and labeling those outside of traditionalism as offenders. Yet even if they are, the Bible gives the church no right to destroy others in the name of God.

How can someone be an enemy of God by trusting in His word? The Apostle Paul was labeled as a heretic and persecuted from city to city. When the religious people of his day found him in a place where they had authority, he was arrested and eventually put to death. Consider the defense of Paul when he stood on trial in **Acts 24:14**

---

[4] Luke 6:26-28

The Purpose of this Book

But this I confess to you, that according to the Way which they call a sect, so I worship the God of my fathers, believing all things which are written in the Law and in the Prophets.

The word 'sect' in this passage is 'hairesis'. It's where we get our word heresy – in fact, many translations use the word heresy instead of sect. The meaning of the word is: men who follow the tenants of their own ways.

The accusation against Paul was that he was a heretic who followed his own tenants. Yet Paul's beliefs didn't come from his own tenants, but from the scriptures themselves. This apostle presented his defense with well-reasoned scriptures, but his accusers tried him on the claim that he was presenting heresy, and never did they disprove anything Paul taught. It boiled down to the fact that Paul was once deceived into believing in the traditional religious establishment, but once he encountered Christ, he understood how that his old way of thinking was overlaying his beliefs on top of scripture, and now he could see that everything in scripture pointed to faith in Christ alone.

Every New Testament principle Paul presented was drawn out of the Old Testament scriptures. Once he understood that everything had to be viewed through Christ, the message of the Old Testament became clear. Grace came before the law, and the law never nullified the promise. The Law came in to reveal man's sin, his complete inability to attain to the glory of God, and this drove mankind to the cross where God's love was fully revealed.

For his entire life, Paul followed the law as closely as any man could. As long as he was able to convince himself that his efforts were earning God's approval, he remained zealous (and blind to his faults). Once Christ revealed Himself to Paul, Jesus showed how Paul was actually fighting against God and that faith was trusting in what Jesus had done and not what religious people should do. That's when Paul looked at all of his accomplishments and said, "I count it all as rubbish." His entire life had been the process of collecting trash; not earning rewards.

With this new understanding, Paul looked at the Law and the Prophets and realized his spirituality had been drawing from human understanding – the achievement mindset. Suddenly it became about Christ. That's when Paul said, by the deeds of the law shall no flesh be justified in His sight. And, if it is by grace, it is no longer of works, otherwise grace would no longer be grace.[5]

This is when Paul abandoned religion and began walking in God's works by faith.[6] Once Paul abandoned religion, he became the enemy of religion. They then began to call him a heretic. He pointed to scripture, but they pointed to their own accusations against Paul. No matter how much Paul tried to shift the focus to the word of God, his opponents built up an accusation against him out of their own assumptions, and not based on what he said or believed. They created the accusation and treated the creation of their own hearts as though it were the heresy of Paul.

Look at any point in human history and you will see true men of faith being accused of heresy because they say, "I believe what was written in the Law and the Prophets." If we believe the Old Testament, it drives us to Christ. If we believe Christ, He points us to the apostles. "You will be my witnesses...the Holy Spirit will guide you into all truth and bring to remembrance all things I said to you."

We now look back at these truths, and the more we grow in our understanding of the Bible, the more our old misconceptions fall away. The problem is, those misconceptions are dearly held beliefs of the church establishment. The church is the body of Christ, but man-centered organizations and establishments divide the body. Jesus said the world would know we are His disciples because of our love (agape) for one another.[7] The Bible says that when the church is focused on Christ and drawing near to Him as their head, it will have unity among the members as the entire body edifies itself in love.[8]

---

[5] Romans 11:6
[6] Ephesians 2:10
[7] John 13:35
[8] Ephesians 4:11-16

The Purpose of this Book

When the church loses focus on Ephesians 4:11-16, it begins to lose unity by turning from Christ and dividing over human disagreements and traditional doctrines. By traditions, I am referring to traditional beliefs introduced by people and not based on the whole word of God. Some estimates indicate that there are more than 30,000 denominations. Many of these are sub-denominations formed when major denominations can't agree. They aren't dividing over Christ. They have created walls of separation that God has clearly taught against, and the walls become the defining tenants of their faith in religion instead of Christ. Then followers of these tenants accuse those who turn back to true faith as being the ones following their own tenants.

When God begins to move people out of the sectarianism mindset, those invested into this way of thinking will call those who seek unity as divisive – not because they have created division, but because they are no longer willing to remain behind the walls of division. Sectarianism is to be divided into sects – groups of people following a person or organization that sets itself under a banner of separation.

We see this strictly condemned in 1 Corinthians. Most of this epistle is dedicated to condemning the divisions being caused by those who are drawing lines of separation based on banners and labels. Consider **1 Corinthians 1:12-13**

> [12] Now I say this, that each of you says, "I am of Paul," or "I am of Apollos," or "I am of Cephas," or "I am of Christ." [13] Is Christ divided? Was Paul crucified for you? Or were you baptized in the name of Paul?

Paul calls them carnal, or fleshly minded, because of the divisions they have created. The people were beginning to divide into groups and excluding those who were not of the right teacher. They looked at Paul, Apollos, and Peter (Cephas) as different sects instead of viewing them as co-labors with different gifts, teachings, and insights.

Today we use terms like Calvinist, Arminianist, Baptist, Presbyterian, Methodist, Reformed, Hardshell, and any number of other labels carnally minded Christians have come up with. Ask yourself this question, "Are these divisions given to us by Christ?" If not, then what is the source?

The more we look to Christ, the more we are drawn outside of the walls of separation, and the more we feel connected to the true body of Christ. Sadly, those who value the walls of separation will view those who step outside of the walls as heretics, and will even call them divisive. Yet is the division coming from those who refuse to be labelled, or is it those who say, "You are no longer of us?"

As God moves people out of the walls of the establishments which defend their doctrines of division, these people are being labeled as evil, heretical, and divisive. And this is happening because we are saying, "We believe what has been stated in the scriptures by God's prophets."

The inspiration for this book was a nationally syndicated broadcast and book tour on many Christian networks called 'The Heresy of the Hyper-Grace Movement.' This book release and campaign calls for believers to fight against the threat of grace teaching in the church.

Like most criticisms, this series defines what people like myself believe as different than we believe, and then tears apart their straw man.

Human driven movements can lead to a new establishment and a new sect, but the movement of God is not so. Following the label can lead to error, but if it's the move of God as it was at the birth of the church and various times in Christian history, it is God calling people out of empty religion and into an eternal walk of faith. Even good movements can lose focus, but that's only because people lose sight of Christ and begin conforming to a new set of rules and boundaries that are not found in scripture.

One thing that affirms my move toward grace is the fact that most of the doctrines criticized I've written about, but I didn't get it from 'a movement'. I came out of a very traditional denomination, and it was the scriptures that compelled me to my conclusions. Some of these conclusions have been affirmed by teaching and books I have come across, but I thought many of the things in my previous books were original. I thought I'd dug out fresh perspectives from the scriptures. They are things I have never been taught or heard taught. I wasn't even aware that others were teaching these things until I came across the criticism of what is now being called 'hyper-grace'.

This begs the question, if I didn't have someone teach me these things, but I clearly saw them in scripture and wrote about them, and now I see that many are being moved to the same conclusions in the church and are also teaching these things, could this be a time when God is moving those who are listening back to faith? People unrelated and unconnected are discovering how they have missed the true focus of faith — trusting in the finished work of Christ. This is affirmation of the move of God.

Let me wrap up this introduction with another question. How can making Christ our focus and trusting in His completed work draw us into error? Isn't temptation, by definition, to take your eyes off of Christ in order to pursue something other than Him? Isn't temptation the quest for fulfillment outside of Christ — not believing God's promise that He is our rewarder, fulfiller, and will give us abundant satisfaction from the river of His pleasures?[9]

One thing to note is that in any denomination, sect, religion, or group you can find fringe beliefs that are outside the truth. Most people have heard of Westboro Baptist church. This is the church that consists mostly of the family members of the 'pastor' and believe they alone are going to heaven. They picket funerals and hold up signs stating that God hates America, soldiers, homosexuals, and proclaim God's doom for all. In an interview, one of the women of the church said that God delights when the wicked die, and though they hold up signs for repentance, there is no way for the sinner to repent because God hates them. While the Bible says that God is love, their belief system teaches that God is hate.

I don't know of a single Baptist church who would agree with the message of Westboro. Yet they are under the banner of Baptist, so is it fair to point to this church and say, "See, this is the result of

---

[9] Hebrews 11:6, Genesis 15:1, Psalm 37:7-8

the Baptist faith and message?" Even if you disagree with the Baptist faith and message, it is an unfair comparison to say this is what the Baptist denominations teach.

In the same way, to point out someone who denies the Bible, uses their own ideas of forgiveness, and follows their own flesh, and say, "See, this is what grace teaches," is an absurd comparison. I know charismatic churches that are very biblical. I know some that are very unbiblical. I know Methodist churches that are spiritually dead. I know other ones that are full of life. Anyone can build a straw-man by pointing to someone within any denomination or group and saying this is what all 'those people' teach. It only shows both ignorance and a desperate attempt to cause division when someone makes blanket claims.

It's because of these straw-men arguments that makes a book like this necessary. So much misinformation is being disseminated and under the guise of 'being jealous for the church.' Our jealousy is carnal. God alone can be jealous for His church. To go on a campaign to turn people against the message of grace by presenting a false view of it must be addressed.

Understanding grace is essential for receiving all things we have been given through Christ. A man-centered merit system religion has no spiritual fruit. The biggest problem in the church is that we don't have a big enough view of God.

Jesus said it best when He stated, "Whatever is born of the flesh is flesh, and whatever is born of the Spirit is spirit."[10] Nothing done through the flesh of human effort can produce anything of the Spirit; therefore, nothing we accomplish is acceptable to God.

Let me give a few quick examples.

Abraham was promised a son by God's power. He believed God, but was distracted from faith when Sarah said, "Maybe you need to do something." It had been years since God gave the promise, and they began to question the idea of grace by faith alone. Then it started to make sense to believe in their own works as an assistance to God. Through human effort, Abraham produced a son by marrying a slave-girl in order to help God along. Sarah was

---

[10] John 3:6

The Purpose of this Book

barren, so it only made sense to the human mind. God never accepted that son as part of His plan. When Isaac was born by Sarah, God called Isaac Abraham's only son.[11]

When Cain and Abel presented their sacrifices to God, Abel provided what God had given him – the cattle of the field, and Cain provided the works of his best effort. He tilled the ground, worked his heart out, and then presented to God the best fruit he had to offer. God rejected Cain's works, but received Abel's. God only receives what He provides.

Jesus said that many will present their good works to God in the last day, but God will reject them.[12] He calls them workers of lawlessness, even though they served in Jesus' name and did the works that Jesus said the church would do. The works came from the fruit of their best efforts, but God rejected them because the works did not come through Him. "I never knew you," was the only reason given for rejecting these religious workers. We walk in the good works God prepared beforehand, not in what we do for God. I'll go into this in detail later in this book.

Through the Law, man provided thousands (if not millions) of sacrifices for God. The Law required the sacrifice, and though men obeyed God, none of these sacrifices were ever received as a payment for sin. The Bible says that it is impossible for these sacrifices to take away sin.[13] The Bible goes on to say that the best these sacrifices could do was to remind the worshipper each year of their sin and need of redemption.[14]

The only sacrifice God ever excepted for sin was what He provided for Himself. As far back as Abraham we are told, "God will provide Himself a lamb." Jesus is then called the Lamb of God, and the Bible says, "You have prepared a body for Me," referring to the birth of Christ, given through the Holy Spirit, which then became the acceptable sacrifice to God.

---

[11] Genesis 22:2
[12] Matthew 7:22-23
[13] Hebrews 10:4
[14] Hebrews 10:3

Throughout scripture, God makes it clear that He accepts what He provides. Man's best work and best gift can never rise above an effort of the flesh.

And this is the message of grace. God has provided to us what is acceptable, and we can now be in perfect fellowship because we relate to God with the gifts He has provided to us. Jesus is the fulfillment of this, for the Bible says, "He came to set the captives free and give gifts to men."[15]

To fully understand this, we need to understand how the Bible defines grace, but grace gets lost in meaningless disputes over petty issues. Differing perspectives are inflated into 'great threats against the church', but few are calling for a reasonable discussion. Instead of saying, "What does the Bible teach and how does your belief fit into this?" we hear nothing but accusations. "You just believe…" or, "Those people believe…" The goal of the enemy is to put Christians on the defensive so the truth is lost from view. As long as brother is warring against brother, the gospel poses little threat against the powers of darkness.

Divisions distract the church from the true message of the gospel. Divide and conquer. Jesus warned that a house divided cannot stand. What are some of the enemy's tactics of division? In the next chapter, we'll explore this question.

---

[15] Ephesians 4:8

The Purpose of this Book

What Causes Division?

Not once have I heard someone come up and say, "What do you believe? Let's look at the scriptures and see how our difference compares to the Bible's teaching." Instead I hear critics of grace picking out quotes that can be misrepresented and using it as a weapon in a meaningless war.

"Do you stand behind this quote?" an author of a grace-rebutting book said. Of course a teacher is going to stand behind a quote from his or her teaching, but they are considering that quote in the context of what they are teaching. They are not considering the way a critic plans to use it. Because God's grace is so relevant and powerful, they are not considering the possibility that an author will frame it in a way that makes grace look like a man-centered gospel.

Confusion arises when people misdefine what grace means. Most of the criticism I hear about grace teaching is based on false assumptions or fleshly ways of thinking. When critics say things like, "This teaching on grace will cause people to sin," and then they go on to criticize their assumptions, it becomes clear that they don't understand how the Bible defines grace. We'll look at the biblical definition of grace in the next chapter.

Grace is not passive. One of the criticisms often repeated makes it clear that critics are looking at grace as though it were a passive, all-encompassing get out of jail free card. The exact same complaint against passive grace is the argument against passive faith. Look at **James 2:18-20**

18 But someone will say, "You have faith, and I have works." Show me your faith without your works, and I will show you my faith by my works.

19 You believe that there is one God. You do well. Even the demons believe-- and tremble!

20 But do you want to know, O foolish man, that faith without works is dead?

Is the Apostle James making the argument that faith doesn't exist? No. He is pointing out that many people claim to have faith, but the evidence proves it isn't the faith given through the Spirit. It's a mere human faith based on a fleshly mind, lived out through a fleshly life. James is not making the argument that faith can only come by works. He's making the argument that if this was truly a work of the Spirit, it would have the works of the Spirit. Walking in faith can't leave a life unaffected.

Many of these people in the church were probably sincere Christians and were truly born through faith in Christ; however, they were drawn back into a fleshly way of thinking where faith was merely a passive intellectual assent that God was real, but they weren't actually looking to the Spirit by faith – trusting in God, His works, and drawing from the life of the Spirit.

Christians can fall back into a fleshly way of thinking. Nearly every epistle in the New Testament addresses believers who have been drawn back into the life of the flesh. Sometimes they are called out for pursuing sin in the flesh. Sometimes they are called out for pursuing works through the flesh. Sometimes they are called out for living out faith through the flesh. Jesus warned, "Whatever is born of the flesh is flesh, and whatever is born of the Spirit is spirit."[16]

Even Christian works, worship, faith, and grace expressed or received through the flesh is flesh. The flesh cannot produce spiritual fruit, so even good works done by human effort is counted as sin in God's eyes. See Matthew 7:22-23.

Criticism against believing in God's grace is based on viewing the work of God through the flesh. Most claim that if someone truly believes in complete grace, it will draw them into sin. This assumption is based on viewing faith through the eyes of the flesh. If you take away rules, regulations, and religious demands, that much freedom will cause people to fall back into sin. Right?

Such a claim is to say that God's Spirit within us is insufficient, and we must bring human effort into faith to complete the work.

---

[16] John 3:6

What Causes Division?

In other words, we have more faith in human religion than in the Spirit of God.

Certainly there will be people who use the ideology of grace as a license to sin. Certainly there will be those who live contrary to the Spirit and claim it's okay because they are under grace. However, consider that throughout church history, people have used religion for selfish gain. This was even true in the era of the apostles. Look at **1 Timothy 6:5**. It begins by explaining how people manipulate scriptures, and ends with:

> [These deceivers argue with] useless wranglings of men of corrupt minds and destitute of the truth, who suppose that godliness is a *means of* gain. From such withdraw yourself.

> The Apostle Paul addresses this again in **2 Corinthians 2:17**
> For we are not, as so many, peddling the word of God; but as of sincerity, but as from God, we speak in the sight of God in Christ.

So do those who manipulate the word of God for personal gain discredit the truth of scripture? To those who are looking at the flesh, yes. But if we have understanding through the Spirit, we also understand that a manipulator doesn't change the heart of truth.

To protect people from the truth in order to take away the opportunity for someone to manipulate it – or others – for personal gain is not spirituality. It's an act of the flesh. We are then taking away the power of God from everyone in order to keep those who do not walk according to the Spirit out of sin. Yet the greater sin is to disbelieve God and snub the Spirit's power to transform our lives.

Every argument against grace is based on fear. Fear that people will fall into sin. Fear that if we give someone too much liberty, they will abandon Christ. When we trust in fear, we step outside of faith. Then those who are walking in faith become a threat, and fear is used as a tool to manipulate religious people into rejecting those who are walking in God's grace by faith.

Why do churches try to turn people against other churches, denominations, and teachings? They don't believe God can give us a discerning heart, or they don't believe the scriptures themselves. They may be sincere, but they are sincerely wrong. One of the things God has said that He hates is when someone sows discord among brethren. Yet religion is notorious for doing this very thing.

Try questioning someone's belief and see what happens? Even if you use scripture to bring a dearly held belief into question, the reaction is often hostility. There is not a quicker way to be labeled as a heretic than to question religious beliefs that are not grounded upon scripture. Hostility arises because there is little security in what we believe. Because we are the shield for our faith instead of faith being our shield, anything that questions our version of faith is considered a threat.

Yet the Bible says that faith is our shield. We should not be protecting faith, but resting in the truth that faith is our protection. Human faith is weak; therefore, it must be protected. Yet true faith comes by hearing the word of God, believing it, and resting upon the assurance of it as our firm foundation. If examining scriptures and reasoning through your doctrines from another perspective is a threat to you, you aren't standing upon God's gift of faith.

Grace changes this. When I held on to traditionally taught beliefs, but didn't have a deeper understanding of the word, I felt the need to stamp out every false teaching. Yet once I found the revelation of the Word of God, I also began to understand how dependent I was upon God for everything. Without the Spirit's revelation, I couldn't understand the heart of faith. Without God's gift of righteousness, I could not be righteous. Without becoming a partaker of God's nature, I cannot be holy. Not one spiritual attribute came to me apart from God's grace.

For this reason, when I see someone who has a different belief, even if that belief is flawed, I no longer view them as a threat. I began desiring for them to receive what I have received. I was suddenly able to have a healthy dialogue with people I once viewed as a threat. I also found that I could guide them into the scriptures that helped them grow, while also examining the scriptures to see if their perspective had merit.

When truth ceases from being a threat, so does falsehood. What is false is exposed by the truth, and every person brings assumptions into their understanding of the word. Most of these assumptions will either be abandoned or sharpened as they grow in the word. But when division separates believers, there is no way to reason the scriptures out.

It's ironic that those who teach against grace are calling for division, while accusing grace-believers of being divisive. This is often done by putting labels on people. Once we label someone, we can put them into a box and cast them away. Those over-emotional people are Charismatics. Those spiritually dead people are Baptists. Or Methodists. Those Lutherans are just trusting in liturgy. Those grace-believers are hyper-gracers.

There are thousands of ways to divide brethren, but only one way to unite. According to Ephesians 4, as we draw into the head, Jesus, we are drawn closer to each other and begin edifying one another in love.

And that is also the message of grace.

Defining Grace

We've discussed why misdefining grace creates confusion, and how divisions distract people from the heart of what grace means, now let's allow the scriptures to define grace.

In simplest terms, grace is the love of God expressed to us through the gifts of His Spirit, given to each believer without merit.

Most of us have heard grace defined as God's unearned favor, but few understand what that means. God is love.[17] Let's take this into a realm we can understand. When you love someone, how to you express that love? You do things for them. You give gifts. How would we feel if someone said, "I can't accept this until I do something to earn it?" Working for your gift would no longer make it a gift. If I'm trying to express my love, someone's merit system would undermine that love.

If I give you a gift, and you won't take it, is it still a gift? It is, but it doesn't benefit you because you haven't received it. If that gift is my expression of love to you, and you say, "I can't take this until I do something to earn it," is it a gift? No. My love would then be forgotten, and both of us are robbed of a relationship based on love.

If I give you a gift and then put rules and expectations upon you, is it a gift? No, then it would be a barter system. What I give would only be a tool to get you to give something to me. That isn't an expression of love. A gift would be something I give for no other reason than the hope of you experiencing the care I have for you. At Christmas and birthdays, I give my children gifts with no expectation – other than the desire of seeing them grow from experiencing my love. No parent looks at a toddler and says, "I gave you a gift. Now you owe me."

We are limited by our humanity, and if we can express love without condition to our children, how much greater is that love from God. What can you give God that He doesn't already own? He

---

[17] 1 John 4:6, 16

created the world and all that is in it. You can't give Him anything. He created your life, gave you talents and abilities, so what can you offer that didn't first originate with Him?

There is nothing you can give or do for God that He needs. In fact, those who serve God often miss the fact that He steps in to give them success so they can feel the satisfaction of expressing love back to Him. It's never about what you do for God, but how you experience the relationship of love He is inviting you to be a part of.

This is as close as we can get to God's love with a human illustration. We can share mutual love with people because we are on the same level. We are both human and can relate on an equal plain. This is not so with God. Mankind is incapable of loving God without God first pouring His love into man's heart.[18]

Every command in scripture where we are called to love God, it is the word 'agape'. Agape is always the love of God. It is never the love of man. When human love is explained in scripture, it is the Greek word 'Philia'. Philia is warm affection and friendship type of love. The Greeks also had another word for love, 'eros'. Eros was sexual love, or physical attraction. The Bible never uses the word eros as love, but it still serves to put things into perspective.

When the Bible calls us to love God with all our heart, mind, soul, and strength, the word is 'agape'. This tips us off to an important truth. A life in the flesh can never fulfill the most basic commands of the Bible. Jesus said that all the commands of scriptures are based on two basic commands: love (agape) God with all your being, and love (agape) your neighbor as yourself.

If this is true, then it is impossible for anyone to keep any command of the law, Old or New Covenants, by personal effort. The best you have to offer God is philia – human friendship. The best you have to offer God is the flesh and human effort based on the works of the flesh. This is why the Bible states in **Romans 3:20:**

> Therefore by the deeds of the law no flesh will be justified in His sight, for by the law *is* the knowledge of sin.

---

[18] Romans 5:5, 1 John 4:19

The best the law can do is reveal to you your incapability of rising up to the love of God. And herein is the wonderful message of grace. Here is where grace begins its work in the Christian's life. Look at **Romans 5:5-6**

> 5 Now hope does not disappoint, because the love of God has been poured out in our hearts by the Holy Spirit who was given to us.
>
> 6 For when we were still without strength, in due time Christ died for the ungodly.

This should be our first clue on the purpose of grace. Before I can even love God, God has to pour His love into my heart. Before I can love my neighbor or any fellow believer, God's agape love must first be poured into my heart. This is why Jesus said, "By this shall all men know you are My disciples, because of your love (agape) for one another."

Human love can only go so far. Human love is self-serving, and when self is threatened, human love fails. When a fellow believer is unlovable or has a less than desirable personality, human love fails as our flesh conflicts with that person.

Let me give an example. A fellow Christian began attending church, and he had a personality that conflicted with a lot of people. I have to be honest, I didn't care much for him either. At first, I struggled to get along with him, but knowing the scripture's command that I must love my brother, I began to question how to do this. I could not love him with philia love, for my flesh did not like his personality. But I'm not called to love with philia, but agape. God's love placed within my heart is the power of God to love that person.

I began asking God to help me view him as a brother. I then began to focus on the areas we had in common. He loved the scriptures, he loved God, and he had a passion for sharing what he was learning. As I focused on his spirit and our relationship in Christ, I also began to find areas where we could get along. I began to love him as a child of God, not as a buddy. We had many discussions and as I focused on the good I saw in him from God, I also began to lose sight of the things that once annoyed me. Before long, those things were all but forgotten and the agape love of God, as it completed its work between us, it also gave birth to philia love. It wasn't long before we were friends and brothers in Christ.

That is what grace does. The agape of God loved him even when I could not. Then the agape of God changed me and removed the barriers between us.

Grace begins with the gift of agape. That agape gives the church the supernatural power to love one another, regardless of personal differences. Wars and fightings begin when human desires are lifted up and agape is neglected. Disputes fall from view when God's love becomes the focus. Believers can look for God's love in the heart of their brethren, and use God's love given to them to overcome human conflict and selfishness. But wait, there's more. And it won't even cost you $19.95 plus shipping.

Everything in the Christian life is received through the grace of God. Anyone who loses sight of this truth falls into performance based religion and a false merit system.

I'll let you in on a secret. There is nothing you can give God that He will accept that does not first originate from His grace expressed toward you. Your love for God must first be given to you by God through the Spirit. Your holiness is a gift of God. Your works were prepared beforehand by God for you to walk in.[19] God is not concerned with what you do for Him, but whether you are abiding in what He has given to you.

Grace teaches that you are not accepted because of what you have done, but what Christ has done. Grace teaches that you aren't loved because of what you do, but because God is love. Sanctification is when God sets us apart for Himself, not when we set ourselves apart for Him. Even faith is given to every person and not something that originates from the human heart.[20] Consider the words of **1 Corinthians 4:7**

---

[19] Ephesians 2:10
[20] Romans 12:3

For who makes you differ *from another*? And what do you have that you did not receive? Now if you did indeed receive *it*, why do you boast as if you had not received *it*?

This is the heart of grace. What do you have that you didn't receive? You aren't doing anything for God; you are receiving what God has given you.

Those who believe in God's grace are declaring that they believe in the completed work of Christ. There is nothing we can do to add to Christ's completed work. Anything we bring to the table is corrupted by the flesh and cannot enter into the realm of the Spirit. The Christian life is then about abiding in what Christ has done. Even our works were finished before the foundation of the world.[21] Our good works are merely to walk by faith in God's works that He prepared beforehand that we should walk in them (see Ephesians 2:10).

Grace is the love of God, packaged into many spiritual gifts, and given to us so we can experience fellowship with Him and see the amazing power of God made manifest in us – the ones who have no power in ourselves. Works are the gifts of God. God prepared the path. God prepared the works. God accomplishes His work. Then God rewards us as though it were our work simply because we trusted in His works enough to walk by faith.

What do you have that you have not received? Nothing. Yet God has promised to reward us for being receivers of His works. Faith in His grace is the gospel.

Grace says that everything good comes from God's hand as a gift to His children. Grace says that I look expectantly to Him as my Provider, Healer, Righteousness, Holiness, and Life. Grace says that none of these come from me, but all are gifts of God, received by faith. Consider the amazing promise of **Hebrews 11:6**

But without faith *it is* impossible to please *Him*, for he who comes to God must believe that He is, and *that* He is a rewarder of those who diligently seek Him.

---

[21] Hebrews 4:3

Defining Grace

Why does God reward us? For what we do? For what we don't do? No. We have faith in His grace. You can spend your life in sacrifice to God and it profit you nothing. Faith is to look expectantly to God and trust in Him. We seek Him because He rewards us with every spiritual and physical blessing. God is pleased when you have faith in His grace. Religion can't provide what God has already given.

Critics of this teaching claim that grace will cause us to sin, but this cannot be true. Understanding grace causes us to look expectantly to Christ so we are partakers of His nature. I cannot sin if I am looking to Christ. Sin only comes when we take our eyes off of Christ and look to something other than Him for fulfillment. How can looking to Christ draw me into sin? To make this claim is to blaspheme His name.

We can always find someone who is living according to the flesh while claiming that God accepts their life of sin. Can you see how this is not faith in God? Pursuing the flesh while claiming it is grace is foolishness. In the same way, trying to work out your salvation by human effort is also foolishness. In fact, to turn your heart away from receiving of Christ's completed work to produce your own righteousness by human effort is just as much of a sin as pursuing lust to produce your own satisfaction. One is a hollow shell of religion, and the other is a hollow shell of gratification.

The Bible says that to be fleshly minded is death, but to be spiritually minded is life and peace. To use dead flesh for religious purposes only produces dead works. To use the dead flesh for selfish gain or lust also produces dead works.

To be spiritually minded is to look expectantly to Christ for life and everything of the Spirit. Take to heart the word of God in **2 Corinthians 3:14-18**

> [14] But their minds were blinded. For until this day the same veil remains unlifted in the reading of the Old Testament, because the *veil* is taken away in Christ.
> [15] But even to this day, when Moses is read, a veil lies on their heart.
> [16] Nevertheless when one turns to the Lord, the veil is taken

away.

¹⁷ Now the Lord is the Spirit; and where the Spirit of the Lord *is*, there *is* liberty.

¹⁸ But we all, with unveiled face, beholding as in a mirror the glory of the Lord, are being transformed into the same image from glory to glory, just as by the Spirit of the Lord.

This passage is drawing a comparison between those who try to please God through the deeds of the law to those who turn to Christ. Keep in mind that this was written by the Apostle Paul, a man who was once a Pharisee and dedicated to the Old Testament Law. Yet once his veil was removed, he used the Old Testament to reveal Christ. It isn't the Old Testament that blinds people with the veil. It is those who miss Christ. People who were stuck in the 'I must please God by what I do' read the Old Testament and their performance based religion became a veil. But those who turned to Christ had the veil removed. Then they could see the truth of God throughout the Old Testament because they understand it all pointed to the work of Christ.

When someone turns to Christ, the cross becomes the light which reveals the truth spread throughout the Old Testament. Without the cross, the Old Testament is merely a book of condemnation. That condemnation is removed once we turn to Christ, for He fulfilled the law on our behalf. The foundation of grace can be clearly seen in **Romans 8:3-4**

³ For what the law could not do in that it was weak through the flesh, God *did* by sending His own Son in the likeness of sinful flesh, on account of sin: He condemned sin in the flesh,

⁴ that the righteous requirement of the law might be fulfilled in us who do not walk according to the flesh but according to the Spirit.

Did you know that the law was fulfilled in you? It is – once you enter into Christ and He in you! Those who try to fulfill the law are walking according to the flesh. They are trying to do through human effort what Christ has already done. It is a denial of Christ's work to try to fulfill the law.

Do you see the wonderful message of grace? You were incapable of fulfilling the law because the flesh is incapable of rising to the level of God's perfection. Therefore, Christ fulfilled the law on your behalf, and then God credits you as being a fulfiller of the law because of your trust in Christ.

The law is fulfilled in you, not because of any effort on your part, but because you looked to Christ and received His gifts of the Spirit. Now the law has been fulfilled in you simply because you believed God.

Let's conclude this chapter by looking at a church whose people were persuaded to mix human effort with grace. The Bible says, "You have fallen from grace," because they believed in teachers who said faith was Jesus plus keeping the law. This chapter begins with, "Who has bewitched you that you should not obey the truth?" The heart of grace is then taught in **Galatians 3:2-7**

> 2 This only I want to learn from you: Did you receive the Spirit by the works of the law, or by the hearing of faith?
> 3 Are you so foolish? Having begun in the Spirit, are you now being made perfect by the flesh?
> 4 Have you suffered so many things in vain-- if indeed *it was* in vain?
> 5 Therefore He who supplies the Spirit to you and works miracles among you, *does He do it* by the works of the law, or by the hearing of faith?--
> 6 just as Abraham "believed God, and it was accounted to him for righteousness."
> 7 Therefore know that *only* those who are of faith are sons of Abraham.

This message is just as important today. The church has little problem with saying we are saved by grace through faith, but then works replaces faith for the rest of the journey. Yet the Bible expressly contradicts this idea. The Christian life is lived the exact same way we are born again – by trusting fully in Christ. It is foolish to begin by faith and then substitute works by human effort (the flesh) in place of faith.

False faith says that grace gives you the power to keep the law. True faith is exactly what we just read – the law is already fulfilled in us who trust in Christ. The person who is focused on Christ can do nothing other than to walk in obedience. The person focused on the law or human works cannot be in obedience regardless of how religious or sincere they are. They are declaring that they don't trust in Christ's completed work; therefore how can they please God? Without faith this is impossible.

Take a second look at verse 4 above. Does God do the miraculous because we do the works of the law? No! It is by the hearing of faith. Hearing – not doing. Faith comes by hearing the word of God.[22] The word proclaims the work of Christ, we hear that word and its promises, and because we believe, we enter those promises by faith. Then God credits us with the benefits as though we have fulfilled the law simply because we trust in the completed work He has accomplished through Christ.

The example of this truth is Abraham. When Abraham heard God's call, the law had not yet been delivered. God revealed grace through Abraham, then sent the people through the desert of the law, and they emerged from the law by seeing the promise of grace again. The law revealed the power of God's grace.

When God credited Abraham with righteousness, what was it that Abraham believed? Sarah was barren and beyond child-bearing years. God said that He would produce a son through Sarah, and this would be the son of promise. Abraham believed God's promise of what he desired of God. Abraham wasn't doing anything religious, works based, or spiritual. He merely believed God's promise of the impossible. Then God established the promise and gave Abraham God's own righteousness.

Abraham made many mistakes, but God never judged him. There were consequences, but the promise was never withdrawn, nor was Abraham ever counted as anything but righteous.

---

[22] Romans 10:17

Defining Grace

One critical mistake Abraham made was trying to help God. Years went by and people began questioning God's promise. Abraham was drawn into doubt, and then when Sarah came up with a solution, Abraham jumped on it. "Maybe you should marry this servant girl. This is the only way the promise can be fulfilled."

It was a reasonable suggestion by human standards. Of course it would not have been miraculous for a young servant girl to produce a child, but Abraham agreed. Through human effort, Abraham tried to use his works to produce God's promise. He produced a child named Ishmael, and God rejected the works of Abraham. The consequences of using human effort to produce the works of God still haunt Abraham's descendants today.

Yet God did not withdraw His promise. Abraham never ceased to trust in God. He stumbled and sinned by an act of disbelief, but God revisited him with the assurance of the promise. Sarah became pregnant and Isaac, the son of promise, was born.

Though both Ishmael and Isaac were living with Abraham, God said, "Take Isaac, your only son." The works of Abraham were never acknowledged by God.

Your works are the same way. There are many who doubt God's power to do the miraculous and will tell you that you must use personal effort to accomplish the works of God, but in the end, God will only acknowledge the works He has produced by promise. Anything you do for God is of the flesh and will be left outside of your relationship with God. Everything God does is by promise and received through faith. God not only credits you with righteousness when you believe Him, but God also accomplishes the miracle of transforming you into a son of promise.

Look again at **Galatians 3:5:**

Therefore He who supplies the Spirit to you and works miracles among you, *does He do it* by the works of the law, or by the hearing of faith?

Are you so foolish that you believe God can rescue you from your sins by faith, but now He is incapable of accomplishing this miracle among you – a transformed life? The Bible promises that as we behold Christ, by faith looking to Him for the power of the Spirit, we are transformed into His likeness. Yet many will claim that God's promise must be helped along by human effort.

All efforts from your abilities must remain outside of the promise, and they can never produce in our lives what God has reserved for Himself to produce through the miracles of the Spirit. Faith in God's grace is miraculous, but it only comes through the Spirit. As you believe, you look expectantly to Christ and receive. Your efforts can only get in the way of God's work. You can never help Him along.

The Myth of Hyper-Grace

The problem with grace is not that it's 'hyper'. The problem is that many have such a small view of God that they limit grace to human understanding.

Webster defines 'hyper' as: extremely active.

The concept of hyper-grace is the idea that people are overemphasizing grace. It is said that hyper-grace believers are extremely focused on grace or have taken God's grace to excess. Keep in mind that it is God who said, "Eye has not seen, nor ear heard, nor has the heart imagined the things that God has in store for those who love Him."[23] The passage where this is taught goes on to explain that even though the human mind can't imagine the depth of God's gifts, it also says that God *has* revealed these things to us by giving us the mind of Christ. God also said that He will do abundantly more than we think or ask.[24] We'll examine this promise shortly.

Think for a moment about the promises of God. His love and grace is abundantly above what the human mind can imagine. The deeper we grow in the Spirit, the more these things are revealed to us, but until we are viewing life through the eyes of the Spirit, these things are hidden from our eyes.

I challenge you to read the Bible from cover to cover and make note of each time God gives a promise that man did not receive because of unbelief, and note each time God questions man's lack of faith. Let's borrow an example from the Old Testament.

King Solomon had a servant named Jeroboam. Jeroboam had no claim to any throne, no authority, and no wealth or power. Solomon fell into idolatry and abandoned the wisdom of God. After ignoring God's call to return to righteousness, God then proclaimed that all but one tribe of Israel would be stripped from his kingdom.

---

[23] 1 Corinthians 2:9
[24] Ephesians 3:20

The Levites were priests and considered a neutral tribe, but the other eleven tribes were part of the king's rule. Only Judah would remain with Solomon's sons, and this was because God promised King David that his children would sit on the throne until Christ came. Now look at **1 Kings 11:29-31**

> 29 Now it happened at that time, when Jeroboam went out of Jerusalem, that the prophet Ahijah the Shilonite met him on the way; and he had clothed himself with a new garment, and the two *were* alone in the field.
> 30 Then Ahijah took hold of the new garment that *was* on him, and tore it *into* twelve pieces.
> 31 And he said to Jeroboam, "Take for yourself ten pieces, for thus says the LORD, the God of Israel:'Behold, I will tear the kingdom out of the hand of Solomon and will give ten tribes to you.

God has just declared the impossible. A servant would now become king. Only God could have made this happen. Even if a nation divided, they would take the wealthy and powerful to make into a king, not a servant of the king they were rebelling against. God's word prevailed, Jeroboam became king, and even though he had seen the power of God, he still did not believe. He could have been a great king, and God promised to establish him with a strong throne if he trusted in the Lord, but look at Jeroboam's decision in **1 Kings 12:26-28**

> 26 And Jeroboam said in his heart, "Now the kingdom may return to the house of David:
> 27 "If these people go up to offer sacrifices in the house of the LORD at Jerusalem, then the heart of this people will turn back to their lord, Rehoboam king of Judah, and they will kill me and go back to Rehoboam king of Judah."
> 28 Therefore the king asked advice, made two calves of gold, and said to the people, "It is too much for you to go up to Jerusalem. Here are your gods, O Israel, which brought you up from the land of Egypt!"

The Myth of Hyper-Grace

The amazing work of God meant nothing to Jeroboam, so he felt that he must do something to preserve his kingdom. God may have done the miraculous to give him the throne, but surely God wouldn't have the power to preserve the throne. Out of fear of losing control, Jeroboam abandoned the promise of God and tried to establish himself by human effort.

This is the challenge every person born of God must overcome. We see God's power to do as He said, but then we don't believe He is able to fulfill His word completely. For this reason, people fall back on their own resources in order to do what we don't believe God can or will do.

Not one time in the Bible do we find someone who believed God too much. Never do we see someone take faith to the extreme. Never does God say, "I didn't mean you to believe Me to that extent." However, many times we see people fall short only because they couldn't walk by faith. How many times did Jesus say, "Why did you doubt?" or "O you of little faith?"

When someone tosses out the term hyper-grace, it's like saying, "You people believe too much. You've taken grace beyond our comprehension, and we believe that to be dangerous."

Is it possible to believe God too much? If God declares, "My grace is sufficient. When you are weak, My strength is perfected in you," is it truly faith to then say, "No, no. Believing in God's transforming power is too hyper?"

Of course, not one person who accuses others of hyper-grace would say they are telling others not to believe, but in reality this is exactly what this means. To trust fully in Christ's completed work of grace is to believe God will do what He said He would do. It's the Spirit who transforms those who abandon human effort and look to Christ alone. It is Jesus who said, "Be it to you according to your faith."

Are we to become New Testament Jeroboams? God has the power to bring us into His kingdom, but now we must do something to finish the work for Him?

Many claim that to believe in grace causes people to sin. We'll address this in detail in the next chapter, but let's stop for a moment to see what the Bible teaches on this. Where does the strength to resist sin come from? By our rules, human effort, and religious regulations? By trying to fulfill the law by personal effort? Let's let God explain the answer to this question. **Ephesians 3:16-20**

> [16] that He would grant you, according to the riches of His glory, <u>to be strengthened with might through His Spirit in the inner man,</u>
> [17] that Christ may dwell in your hearts through faith; <u>that you, being rooted and grounded in love,</u>
> [18] may be able to comprehend with all the saints what *is* the width and length and depth and height--
> [19] to know the love of Christ which passes knowledge; <u>that you may be filled with all the fullness of God.</u>
> [20] Now to Him who is able to do exceedingly abundantly above all that we ask or think, <u>according to the power that works in us,</u>
> [21] <u>to Him *be* glory</u> in the church by Christ Jesus to all generations, forever and ever. Amen.

Look at the sections I highlighted as it pertains to this discussion:

-Our inner man is strengthened through the power of His might.
-Christ within us grounds us in His love.
-He overflows us with the fullness of God.
-It is His power that works in us.
- He does exceedingly abundantly above what we ask or think.
-It's all so that He alone gets the glory.

The root of the problem is pride, but the root of the answer is faith. Pride calls us to work through human effort so we can proclaim, "Look what I have done for you, God." Yet scripture teaches, "No flesh will glory in His presence." This is reiterated at the end of the above passage. Our victory and life of power is so

Jesus gets the glory. It isn't you keeping the law or accomplishing anything through human effort. It is about God's power, strength, and works so that God is glorified.

In this passage is the very essence of grace. Grace is God's love, packaged into spiritual gifts for you. His power is His gift to you. His love is His gift to you. The overflow of God's fullness is God's gift to you. And the promise is that these things are exceedingly abundantly supplied above what we can ask or even imagine (think). Perhaps this is hyper-grace, but it is God who declared these to be abundantly above what the human mind can comprehend.

Let's continue on to see another example of God's hyper-promise of grace. Look at **Romans 5:17**

> For if by the one man's offense death reigned through the one, much more those who receive abundance of grace and of the gift of righteousness will reign in life through the One, Jesus Christ.

Grace is received in abundance? Hyper-grace? If hyper-grace is to believe in God's promise of excessive abundance, then yes. If someone is claiming that we are taking God's promise outside the limits of scripture, then they simply don't understand what we have been promised in scripture.

Consider the comparison being made. Sin came through Adam and reigned through all men. Now Christ has come to end that curse of sin. Not only does He cause grace to reign, but he causes it to reign abundantly more than what the curse took away. Sin cursed, but grace provides abundantly more than sin could ever destroy.

In every promise God has only one requirement – that you have faith in what He has done and given. Those who make the claim that trusting excessively is hyper-grace are overlooking this important truth. As one critic put it, "We have to do our part. We don't just sit on our laurels and say God has done it all."

Let's see how the Bible answers this objection. Look now at **Romans 5:1-2**

The Myth of Hyper-Grace   35

¹ Therefore, having been justified by faith, we have peace with God through our Lord Jesus Christ,
² through whom also we have access by faith into this grace in which we stand, and rejoice in hope of the glory of God.

According to the Bible, what is our part? According to Jesus, what is our part? When the religious people asked, "What must we do to work the works of God?" Jesus said, "This is the work of God, that you believe on the one God has sent," referring to Himself.

Romans above affirms this truth. How are you justified? By faith – trusting in the works of God. The author of a recently released book said that this applies only to justification. He said that we are legally justified, but hyper-grace goes beyond this.

So does the scriptures. Not only are we justified, but we now have access by faith into the grace of God by which we stand. Not only justified, but we also stand in the fullness of God's presence, fully accepted and rejoicing in the hope of His glory. It's all about His glory and our faith in what we have been given.

Notice that works are not mentioned. We'll talk about works in the Christian life later, but works do not make us right with God. Keeping the law doesn't make us right with God. Going through a perpetual system of repentance does not make us right with God. We rejoice because we are already right with God because of what He has done. By faith we stand in His presence, rejoicing in the amazing grace He has given. We are rejoicing in God, focused on Him, receiving His power, and He has promised to be the transforming work in our lives.

I believe this is true; therefore, I stand by faith in the grace by which I stand. Any other foundation is mere human effort and is destined for the spiritual trash heap. It serves no other purpose than to blind us with human pride so we are focused on what we are doing and cannot see what God has done – and has given us as a gift of His grace.

Many are now claiming that this teaching is untethered from scripture. One critic put it this way. It's like someone being filled like a balloon. They rejoice in grace, but they become untethered from scripture and float away into heresy.

Judge for yourself. Do the above scriptures teach that God empowers us to keep the law or Christian procedures? Or does it teach us that we are receivers of God's works and we rejoice in what He has done? Do the scriptures teach us that grace is only for justification? Or is grace God's expression of love through every spiritual gift? Is rejoicing in God's works untethered from scripture? Is grace about presenting our works, or receiving His works? Is it about what I do? Or is it about glorifying God by rejoicing in what He has done?

My hope is that as you proceed through this book, the scriptures we examine compel you to the truth that the only conclusion is that we underestimate the power of grace. We don't trust God enough. Yet as we learn to trust and receive, God shows His power within us to change our lives from fleshly minded sin to spiritually minded grace. It is God who rescues you by His power. It is not about your ability to resist temptation.

All things are of God, and we grow into maturity by learning to trust fully in the grace we have received. Whether we are tempted to sin, or tempted to establish our own righteousness and works, both are acts of the flesh. Grace is not about thinking we have the power to do good, but instead, it's about God's good transforming us through the inner man. As our faith in His power is established, our outward behavior is also transformed according to His inner working.

Myth - Grace Promotes Sin

A national broadcast scoffed at grace stating, "This heresy is causing pastors to leave their wives and marry their secretaries." He then apparently remembered that all the recent church scandals involve people who teach a mixture of grace and law, so he corrected himself by saying, "This is happening in other churches, but now hyper-grace is giving them an excuse for their sin."

How is it that all the examples of rampant sin and church scandals are among legalistic and semi-legalistic churches, but grace is to blame for their sins? Have you heard of Charles Templeton? He was a pastor and the co-founder of Youth for Christ with Billy Graham. He didn't understand grace, and the burden of measuring up to the standard of God became too much for him. He missed the beauty of fellowship by grace and when the burden became too great, he renounced his faith and was an avowed atheist until his death in 2001. Sam Kinison was a pastor turned atheist comedian who made his living on mocking Christ. Religion failed him because he was focused on what he did for God and not what Christ did for him. Church history is sprinkled with such men. What I have never seen is someone who truly trusted in the completed work of Christ who failed to walk in victory.

Let's stop for a moment and look at sin in the church and why it occurs. It's important to gain the right perspective because sooner or later someone who claims to be living in grace will justify a sinful lifestyle. Then everyone will point to them and say, "See. This is the fruit of grace/hyper-grace."

Never mind that church history is filled with people who taught righteousness by works and fell into adultery and other sins. Off the top of my head, I can think of six nationally known preachers who fell into sexual sin within the last decade or so. None were grace teachers. Two were well known for condemning people and groups who struggled with sexuality.

The heart of the problem is that no person is immune to sin. The most vulnerable among us are the ones who think they stand by their own merits and power. Those who stand on a platform and point a downward finger of condemnation are at a higher risk than those who know they are weak. Consider the words of **Galatians 6:1-2**

> [1] Brethren, if a man is overtaken in any trespass, you who *are* spiritual restore such a one in a spirit of gentleness, considering yourself lest you also be tempted.
> [2] Bear one another's burdens, and so fulfill the law of Christ.

Aha! There's the word 'law'. Isn't this saying we must fulfill the law? According to what we read in a previous chapter, we fulfill the law by being in Christ. Look at the message of this passage. The spiritual are those who are abiding in the Spirit, and they are called to do two things. Take heed to themselves because they are no less capable of falling than the person they are reaching out to. Second is to restore the person in a spirit of gentleness. Gentleness, not condemnation. Not pointing a finger down at them and saying, "You are condemned."

Each week I pass a church whose sign always presents the gospel in a negative fashion. Every person who passes is condemned for not being in church, being proud, having secret sins, not reading their Bible, and what they do or don't do. Is this really the gospel message? And does the message of condemnation work?

Gentleness is to express the love of God we have been given to another person as we help restore them into the love and acceptance of God. The church has the tendency to shoot the wounded instead of restoring them. The reason people point a condemning finger is because they are unaware of how dependent they are upon Christ. I am only right with God because God has rescued me. I can only be spiritual because God has shown me how to receive His gifts of grace. My goal is not to show people how sinful they are, but how to experience the righteousness of God.

When I understand that my personal righteousness is nothing, I have no desire to look down on your sins. If I take my eyes off of Christ, I am just as vulnerable to my fleshly passions as the person living in sin.

People will fall into sin – even though they know better. It has always been a part of humanity and will continue to be so until this age has come to an end. Before you point a condemning finger at someone's failures, the Bible warns to take heed to yourself, for you also can be tempted. And them moment we become dependent upon self-righteousness we are set up for a fall. The Bible even addresses this in Proverbs 16:18, "Before destruction is pride, and before a fall is a haughty spirit."

The person who stands in pride is standing upon their own strength. Pride is stripped from its power as we begin to understand the words of Paul, "In myself, no good thing dwells." Pride has no place to take hold in the life that is looking to God for every good and spiritual attribute in their life.

Let's look at another passage that helps put the idea of sin and grace into perspective. Look at **2 Peter 3:14-18**

¹⁴ Therefore, beloved, looking forward to these things, be diligent to be found by Him in peace, without spot and blameless;

¹⁵ and consider *that* the longsuffering of our Lord *is* salvation-- as also our beloved brother Paul, according to the wisdom given to him, has written to you,

¹⁶ as also in all his epistles, speaking in them of these things, in which are some things hard to understand, which untaught and unstable *people* twist to their own destruction, as *they do* also the rest of the Scriptures.

¹⁷ You therefore, beloved, since you know *this* beforehand, beware lest you also fall from your own steadfastness, being led away with the error of the wicked;

¹⁸ but grow in the grace and knowledge of our Lord and Savior Jesus Christ. To Him *be* the glory both now and forever. Amen.

This passage is filled with so many truths to glean from. Let me first point out the overarching theme of this short section of Peter's letter to the church. There are people who are led away into error, but we stand firm by steadfastness, and growing in grace and the knowledge of Christ.

Steadfastness comes from the Greek word sterigmos, which means, firm condition. The principle being taught is that we are firmly grounded in Christ and are outside of wickedness – unless we are led away from Christ to put our focus elsewhere. Some are led away by the error of wickedness, but how do we stand firm? By growing in grace and the knowledge of Christ.

Stop for a moment and meditate on this basic truth. Grace is the immunity against error. Growing in grace is to grow through the gifts of God's love, given to us through Christ. Knowledge of Christ is to understand His complete work. This isn't a message of doing to be, but a message that we are already there and should not allow any teaching or temptation to move us away from what we already have in Christ.

A secondary principle is also taught that applies to our discussion. There are people who twist scriptures for their own purposes. They are in the destruction of the flesh, but they attempt to twist the scriptures to suit their own purposes. They take the message of truth, which teaches us the knowledge of grace and Christ, and they twist it into a justification for the flesh.

Keep in mind that the fleshly mind cannot discern the things of the Spirit and cannot understand them, for they are spiritually discerned. Of course there will be people who don't have God's Spirit and attempt to justify themselves by twisting scriptures out of their intended meaning.

If someone who has not been born into the Spirit, doesn't have Christ dwelling within them, and has no discerning of the Spirit, and that person lives a godless life while claiming they are covered by grace, does that make the scriptures false? No. The world will live like the world, and even if they use Christian terms and twisted scriptures, they are still of the world. Without a new spirit, born of God, they cannot live according to the Spirit. This is true whether they are trying to use grace as a license to sin or trying to use works to make themselves righteous.

So what grace critics are doing is pointing to someone who still has a corrupted nature but uses the word 'grace' and then says, "See, they are using hyper-grace to justify their sins." Of course they are. They can do no other. The message of grace can only work in a life that has a new spiritual nature and whose life is in Christ. These same people are in legalistic churches and twisting whatever form of doctrine they are receiving into a self-serving gospel. Some are sincerely trying to justify themselves before God through works of the flesh, while others are drawn to doctrines that they can twist into something that eases their conscience.

A professing Christian who is still of the flesh is not evidence that grace is a false teaching. Grace is spiritual. God's word is spiritual. It can only be applied through a life that is born of the Spirit. Anything else, regardless of how sinful or holy it may appear, is still a life in the flesh.

Don't let someone poison your mind to the gospel by pointing at an unredeemed life. Don't let someone who falls from steadfastness of grace in Christ become justification for you rejecting the clearly taught truth of the completed work of Christ.

Contrary to the claims of those who do not understand grace, the message of grace does not lead people into sin. It leads us away from sin. Pay close attention to the words of **Titus 2:11-15**

> [11] For the grace of God that brings salvation has appeared to all men,
>
> [12] teaching us that, denying ungodliness and worldly lusts, we should live soberly, righteously, and godly in the present age,
>
> [13] looking for the blessed hope and glorious appearing of our great God and Savior Jesus Christ,
>
> [14] who gave Himself for us, that He might redeem us from every lawless deed and purify for Himself *His* own special people, zealous for good works.
>
> [15] Speak these things, exhort, and rebuke with all authority. Let no one despise you.

I love the final words of this section of scripture – let no one despise you. If you trust the gospel fully, people will despise you. Even Christians can get caught into the culture of the day and be persuaded to turn against their brethren. Once someone labels you as an enemy of God, many Christians will feel justified in persecuting you. To not let anyone despise you means to not be deterred from the truth just because you draw criticism.

Notice the sentence that flows from verse 11 to 12. It is the grace of God which teaches you to deny ungodliness and worldly lusts. Not only that, grace also teaches us to live soberly, and godly in this present age – an age that is corrupted and filled with ungodliness. The grace of God working in you creates a zeal for good works. Grace *is* the Christian life.

While critics of grace claim that grace teaches us to sin, God has said that grace teaches us both how to avoid sin, and how to abide in spiritual victory.

It is so simple to understand, but hard to accept unless we stop looking at Christianity through the eyes of the flesh. Human reasoning says that grace is too much freedom. If you give people that much freedom, they will wander away from truth. Human reasoning says that we can't be trusted to have no legal boundaries, for then people will dive into the river of sinful pleasures. We can't trust people not to sin.

There is a fundamental flaw with this way of reasoning. It assumes that the flesh is in control. The law was added because of transgressions (Galatians 3:19), but was only to remain until the Seed of our promise came (Jesus Christ). Before Christ, we were bound to a sinful nature inherited through Adam. When we turn to Christ, the Spirit circumcises that nature out of us and replaces it with a new nature, one born of God, incorruptible, and one that is unaffected by sin.

The old nature had to have the law. Without external restraints, the flesh nature pushed boundaries and looked for any avenue available to gratify itself through lusts. That nature is gone. What grace critics are saying is that they either don't believe God has the power to cut away our sinful nature, or He doesn't have the power to overcome this body of flesh. They don't understand that God leads us by our new nature and grace teaches us to turn from this body of flesh and live according to our new nature given to us by God.

What's more is that according to scripture, the law stirs the passions of the flesh and increases sin. The law produces evil desires in the flesh. The reason is because the law is spiritual, but the flesh is carnal. Since these two can never be in agreement, death reigns through the law. Carefully read **Romans 7:8-13**

8 But sin, taking opportunity by the commandment, produced in me all *manner of evil* desire. For apart from the law sin *was* dead.

9 I was alive once without the law, but when the commandment came, sin revived and I died.

10 And the commandment, which *was* to *bring* life, I found to *bring* death.

11 For sin, taking occasion by the commandment, deceived me, and by it killed *me.*

12 Therefore the law *is* holy, and the commandment holy and just and good.

13 Has then what is good become death to me? Certainly not! But sin, that it might appear sin, was producing death in me through what is good, so that sin through the commandment might become exceedingly sinful.

The failure is not the law. The failure is that the flesh is spurred into rebellion when it is employed as a tool for righteousness. When someone tries to use the law to produce good, they don't find righteousness but sin. And this will always be so, for even if a Christian turns to the law, they are in rebellion against Christ. Christ has fulfilled the law and called us to trust in Him by faith, and then we are credited as having fulfilled the law in Him. To then decide to use the law as a tool to produce righteousness is to disbelieve Christ or to reject what He has already accomplished and offered to us.

Myth – Grace Promotes Sin

We are then trying to usurp the authority of Christ and produce our own righteousness apart from Him. Even if we are sincere, it is still an insult to the spirit of grace.[25] When Christians try to mix law and grace they are still in unbelief of the finished work of Christ and the power of God to accomplish what He said He would do.

Grace cannot lead us into sin, for grace is to be focused on Christ and to be in a constant state of receiving His works by faith. Sin can only occur when we are drawn away from our steadfastness in Him. Works by human effort are not focused on Christ and put us into the arena where we must fight sin from our own strength.

A Christian is not trying to overcome sin. A Christian has already overcome sin. The only thing we can do is invite it back into our lives, where it has no power or dominion other than what we give to it. Since the strength of sin is the law,[26] anyone submitting back under the law is giving power to sin. Grace strips sin of its power, and those under grace have no fear of sin. Let's wrap up this chapter with **Romans 6:11-16**

> [11] Likewise you also, reckon yourselves to be dead indeed to sin, but alive to God in Christ Jesus our Lord.
> [12] Therefore do not let sin reign in your mortal body, that you should obey it in its lusts.
> [13] And do not present your members as instruments of unrighteousness to sin, but present yourselves to God as being alive from the dead, and your members as instruments of righteousness to God.
> [14] For sin shall not have dominion over you, for you are not under law but under grace.
> [15] What then? Shall we sin because we are not under law but under grace? Certainly not!
> [16] Do you not know that to whom you present yourselves slaves to obey, you are that one's slaves whom you obey, whether of sin *leading* to death, or of obedience *leading* to righteousness?

---

[25] Hebrews 10:29
[26] 1 Corinthians 15:56

I realize this chapter has quoted a lot of large blocks of scripture, but I encourage you to read and meditate on these passages. This passage is filled with truth that gives us understanding of grace. What overcomes sin? It's not the law, but grace. Call it hyper-grace if you wish, but it doesn't change the plainly taught truth of scripture. The law empowers sin. Grace defeats it. The weakness of the law is the flesh. The strength of grace is Christ. Do you see how many have the message backwards? It is not grace that leads people into sin, but returning to a religious system that is dependent upon your efforts.

We've already discussed how you are dead to the flesh and raised into Christ. Now look at the concept of 'letting' sin have power. Do not let sin reign. Do not present yourselves as a slave to sin. Do not submit yourself to sin. All of these statements have one thing in common – sin is already dethroned. Sin has no power. Sin cannot reign. Sin may war against your mind, but it can only do so through the flesh. In the Spirit, it has no power. Only by submitting to it and giving it the reins can it have any affect over your life.

Stop trying to defeat sin and start trusting in Christ's completed work. He has already defeated sin, and if you are in Him, righteousness is on the throne. Sin and temptation are bluffers. They bluff you into submission, and those who think they must do something to win are stepping into the mire of human effort. They are stepping out of Christ's victory, and trying to use the weakness of the flesh to defeat the sin that rules the flesh.

Let me point out one final truth in the above passage. Why does sin not have dominion over you? Because you are no longer under the law, but under grace. The law is the strength of sin, but grace is the power of Christ. Grace has already defeated sin.

Do you believe God? Do you trust in your efforts more than the grace of God? Or as the Bible said to the Galatians, "Are you so foolish, having begun in the Spirit, do you now think you are made perfect through the flesh?"

Grace is by the Spirit. Grace is the completed work of Christ and is imparted to those who have faith in Him. The Spirit of God takes the gifts of His grace and applies them to the life who walks by faith. The one who tries to accomplish the Christian life for God is walking according to the flesh and human effort. Religion is filled with Christian terms, but its dependency is on human effort. Living in grace is to believe God and trust that He has the power to perfect us, accomplish His work through us, and keep us out of the temptations of the flesh.

It is grace, trusting in the completed work of Christ, that teaches you how to deny ungodliness and lusts, while also teaching you how to receive His righteousness and every spiritual gift. It's already yours. Grace is God's love, given to you, and applied by faith in His power to fulfill His word.

All else is sin – regardless of how religious it may or may not appear to be.

Myth - Grace Excludes Scriptures

One of the myths against grace was explained this way. "Grace teachers exclude large portions of scripture. They throw out the Old Testament. They throw out the teachings of Jesus by claiming that the only thing that applies are the teachings that came after the cross." One critic went as far as to claim that grace teaching originated from the heresy of Marcion. He said, "Modern grace teachers have gone back to this heresy and are now departing from the faith."

Let's first dispel the idea that grace teaching originated from Marcion. Marcion began a pseudo-Christian sect based on dualism. His dualistic belief was that there was a destructive god and a creative god. The god of the Old Testament was not the same god of the New Testament. He completely rejected the Old Testament and a large portion of the New Testament. He accepted the gospel of Luke and most of Paul's writings, but he rewrote scripture to fit his belief system. He compiled an eleven volume canon of scripture that he used and provided for his followers.

This has nothing to do with grace or modern Christianity. I don't know a single person who believes in the completed work of God's grace who thinks there are two opposing gods. To make such a comparison is absurd and serves no other purpose than to build a straw man that can easily be beaten with the stick of fear. This accusation is not worthy of any more text than I've already written.

What needs more attention is the claim that grace causes people to reject the teachings of Jesus and the Old Testament. This is completely false. The Old Testament is filled with teachings that reveal grace and point to Christ. Using the Old Testament to preach that we are to return to law is contrary to grace, but it isn't the Old Testament that is in conflict, but the assumptions of many legalistic teachers.

What many who believe in Christ's completed work are teaching (myself included) is that all scripture must be viewed through the lens of the cross. This includes both the Old Testament, and the teachings of Jesus.

Many of Jesus' teachings are directed at the New Testament church. This is especially true when He was alone with His disciples. Yet there are times when Jesus used the law to drive people to recognize their inability to keep the law so they felt the full condemnation of the law. Let me give a few examples.

When teaching before the Jewish religious leaders, He forced them to see the full measure of the law. "You have heard it taught, do not commit adultery. But I say to you, if you have looked at a woman and lusted in your heart, you have already committed adultery."

Jesus is not saying that He is bringing in a higher standard for the church. He's not saying the Old Testament believers were only guilty if they commit the physical act, but the church is guilty if they even have a thought. He's revealing to the people that they were guilty of the law – even if the physical act never took place. He's preaching to a crowd who trusted in the law. You think you are fulfilling the law, but that's only because you don't understand the law. It's not merely the physical act, but it also includes the sin of the heart.

He said to hate your brother makes you guilty of murder. Among Him were many who thought they were righteous. They never murdered, but now Jesus is calling them murderers. If you wish someone was dead, you are guilty of murder even if you haven't actually committed the act. And many wished Jesus to be dead since He kept rocking their boat of religion.

Then He directly targeted the religious leaders. They thought they had found a loophole in the law. If they gave a writing of divorcement, they could leave their wives and marry someone else. But the same passage where Jesus talked about lust, he also addressed divorce. Certainly they could divorce if they chose to do so, but this didn't nullify the law. They were still bound by the law to that wife, even if they chose to live apart. To marry after divorce was still adultery.

Jesus isn't creating a higher form of the law under grace. Jesus is pointing out the full measure of the law to those who were under the law. And as the Bible says, the Law condemns everyone who is under the law so that every mouth is silenced and everyone is found guilty before God. See Romans 3:19.

Let me give another example. A rich young ruler came to Jesus and asked what he must do to inherit eternal life. He came to Jesus with the works of the law, and Jesus used the law to dismantle his self-righteousness. Jesus went down the list of commandments, two of which were love (agape) God with all your heart and love (agape) your neighbor as yourself.

As mentioned earlier, this is a loaded command under the law, for man is not capable of agape, and this can only be fulfilled by God's love (agape) being first poured into our hearts. But this man looked at his goodness from a human perspective. He hadn't killed, stolen, or murdered. He hadn't done anyone wrong, at least not that he could remember. So he said, "I've kept these from my youth up."

Really? Why then are you rich and your neighbor poor? How could this man have wealth in abundance while widows were out gleaning the fields for grains that were missed by the reapers? Why is there still beggars at the temple gate? He thought he was justified under the law, so Jesus gave him a larger measure of the law than he was willing to do. "If you will be perfect, sell all you have, give it all to the poor, and come follow Me."

Notice the gospel tucked into this exchange. The real answer was, "Come and follow Me," but first the law must bring our condition into focus. This man loved his wealth and could not measure up to the law. He walked away sorrowful and defeated. His self-righteousness was dismantled, and he was unwilling to become dependent upon Christ alone.

So is Jesus saying that in order to find salvation we must all sell our possessions? Is Jesus teaching righteousness by works? No. Never again do we see Jesus calling people to sell everything they have. We see the call to lose our life in the flesh so that we can receive the life of the Spirit, but this isn't salvation by works. Jesus' goal was to reveal to this law-keeper that he could not keep the law. He thought the law was a list of do's and don't's, but the law actually condemns everything that has not emerged from God's own agape love.

When we understand grace (God's completed work of love, given to us as a gift of His unmerited favor), we can then look at the Old Testament and the teachings of Jesus with understanding. We then can understand that these teachings reveal Christ, reveal the need for Christ, or are examples of the works of Christ. Once we view everything through the cross, the message being taught becomes clear.

When I was a child, we had a game called 'Password'. The game had cards filled with red print, but hidden in the background was a word in blue. It couldn't be seen until it was put behind the lens of the card holder. The holder had a window made of red film. Once the card passed behind that red film, the hidden word was made clear. Until that film was applied, it was impossible to see the hidden message.

This is a great word-picture of the message of grace. This is exactly what the Bible teaches. In times past, the law was viewed only through human understanding and people were incapable of understanding the depths of God. Now that Christ has been revealed, through Him and His blood, we can now see what was once hidden. The New Testament has so many passages that speak of this truth that it's hard to know where to start. Let's begin with **Ephesians 3:8-11**

> 8 To me, who am less than the least of all the saints, this grace was given, that I should preach among the Gentiles the unsearchable riches of Christ,
> 9 and to make all see what *is* the fellowship of the mystery, which from the beginning of the ages has been hidden in God who created all things through Jesus Christ;
> 10 to the intent that now the manifold wisdom of God might be made known by the church to the principalities and

powers in the heavenly *places,*

^{11} according to the eternal purpose which He accomplished in Christ Jesus our Lord,

The Bible says that the natural mind cannot receive the things of God, nor can it understand them.[27] Even a Christian, if they are looking at the things of God through human understanding, are blind to the truths God is revealing through the Spirit.

Look at verse 9 above. The things we now have through Christ were once hidden from the world. These were even hidden from God's people in the Old Testament. They kept ordinances by faith, but they had no understanding of why they were keeping these things and most did not understand how they pointed to the revelation of Christ. These have now been revealed through Christ. The power of God accomplished through Christ, and given to us, has been revealed. But this will not be understood by anyone who looks at scriptures through any lens other than the cross. Any who do not understand the finished work of the cross will not understand what God is revealing. Consider **1 Corinthians 2:6-7**

^{6} However, we speak wisdom among those who are mature, yet not the wisdom of this age, nor of the rulers of this age, who are coming to nothing.

^{7} But we speak the wisdom of God in a mystery, the hidden *wisdom* which God ordained before the ages for our glory,

Wow! Do you realize what you have been given? From the foundation of the world to the birth of the church, the wisdom of God was a mystery. No one looking at life, scriptures, faith, or any other spiritual ideology without looking through the cross cannot see what has been plainly revealed.

Any who are looking at the Bible through the lens of the law are looking at the veil. Yet as we mature in the spirit, we begin to discover God's revelation of all things through Christ. Any wisdom outside of the completed work of Christ (which is the gift of grace) will come to nothing and is merely a distraction from what God

---

[27] 1 Corinthians 2:14

The Myth that Grace Excludes Scriptures

reveals to those who seek Him. This is why Romans 3:20-21 says that the deeds of the law cannot justify us in God's sight, but righteousness apart from the law has been revealed by God. Let's look at one more passage on this topic. **1 Corinthians 2:9-10**

> 9 But as it is written: "Eye has not seen, nor ear heard, Nor have entered into the heart of man The things which God has prepared for those who love Him."
>
> 10 But God has revealed *them* to us through His Spirit. For the Spirit searches all things, yes, the deep things of God.

This goes back to the scriptures teaching that the natural mind cannot receive or understand the things of the Spirit. Humanly speaking, all that God has given and what we have in Christ is incomprehensible to the human mind. What you can imagine, have heard about truth, or has entered into your heart falls desperately short of what God has actually given to us. Yet this scripture doesn't end there. Your earthly mind can't imagine the depths of God's gift, but it has been revealed to us by His Spirit.

Do you see the magnitude of this passage? The depths of spiritual truth cannot come through the mind – it can only be revealed to us through the Spirit. This is why doctrine appears confusing to so many people. This is why many well-meaning Christians condemn grace. They are viewing the gift of God through human understanding, and as long as they approach scripture from the human perspective, they will never discover the richness of God's grace.

When someone views the scriptures through the cross, they clearly understand what is being taught and how it applies to faith. They are then able to discern between what was intended to drive people who are outside of faith to the cross, and what is intended to teach us how to walk in grace. What the natural mind calls heresy is merely being viewed and interpreted through the flesh.

How can grace not lead people into sin? That much freedom can only become a temptation to indulge, right? To the natural mind, that would be true, for they are viewing life through the flesh. But the spiritually minded sees the reality of life in the Spirit.

The Myth that Grace Excludes Scriptures

The chains of the law fall away and no longer drag us down. We then are free to pursue Christ and life in the Spirit without distraction. Instead of looking at grace as an occasion of the flesh, we now view it as freedom to thrive in the Spirit. It's only viewed as temptation by the natural mind which is still focused on sin, and because they are always conscious of sin, it is always a distraction. Therefore, the natural mind assumes freedom will become overwhelming since spiritual life is being viewed through the lens of the flesh.

Let's begin wrapping this chapter up through the perspective of **Romans 8:5-6**

> 5 For those who live according to the flesh set their minds on the things of the flesh, but those *who live* according to the Spirit, the things of the Spirit.
> 6 For to be carnally minded *is* death, but to be spiritually minded *is* life and peace.

This isn't only speaking to the non-Christian. If you view scripture through the flesh, you will see the condemnation of death. The Bible says that those who read the Old Testament from the perspective of the Law have a veil over their face, and that veil remains until they come through Christ.[28] The Bible also calls the Old Testament Law the law of sin and death.[29] It is for this reason people miss grace. They are blinded by the veil of the law, and because they are looking at the Bible as a law of works, they see sin and death. Then the Bible appears to be about avoiding sin and trying to escape death.

Those who view the scriptures through the lens of grace by the cross see life and peace. Sin loses its stronghold, for life displaces death. They enjoy fellowship with God because they only see peace with God. Condemnation has died with the flesh.

What the naturally minded Christian doesn't grasp is that grace isn't a deception that draws us toward sin. Grace is life that

---

[28] 2 Corinthians 3:14
[29] Romans 8:2

The Myth that Grace Excludes Scriptures

draws us into a deeper fellowship with God. Then we go on to maturity instead of re-laying the foundation of repentance.[30]

You can never grow into maturity by looking to your own works, righteousness, sin, law, or any religious practice that is dependent upon what you do for God. Maturity comes by drawing closer to Christ, and believing in the love He has for us so we have the faith to receive His good works.

Rather than excluding the scriptures that 'don't fit the grace message' as some claim, faith compels us to believe in the truth that we have been given all things that pertain to life and godliness,[31] and that everything comes through the completed work of Christ. This includes interpreting scriptures. There is not one scripture I disagree with – Old or New Testament. However, God has given us a standard by which we must view scripture.
Romans 8:3-4

> [3] For what the law could not do in that it was weak through the flesh, God *did* by sending His own Son in the likeness of sinful flesh, on account of sin: He condemned sin in the flesh,
> [4] that the righteous requirement of the law might be fulfilled in us who do not walk according to the flesh but according to the Spirit.

The righteous requirement of the law can only be received through the Spirit. If the flesh could not keep the law in the Old Testament, it still cannot keep the law today. However, what the law required of you and I has already been fulfilled in us, because we are standing in the grace of God by faith. Jesus completed the work, and we now stand by faith. Every scripture must be viewed through this lens.

I used to think grace was one of the doctrines of the Christian faith, but now I understand it is the keystone that holds everything in place. Grace is the foundation everything is built upon. Once I

---

[30] Hebrews 6:1
[31] 2 Peter 1:3

The Myth that Grace Excludes Scriptures

understood this, the scriptures burst with life in the Spirit. Until this realization dawns in your heart, grace will be viewed as a threat.

I realize that people won't say those exact words, "Grace is a threat," but this is the reality of a misunderstanding of grace. If your definition of grace points to anything but the completed work of Christ, it is just the law repackaged for modern times. If grace is anything man-dependent, it is no longer the grace of God. See Romans 11:6. Grace + human effort = law.

Hopefully you can see that grace does not teach us to deny scriptures, but rather is the lens that make God's revelation in the scriptures come alive. Any interpretation outside of grace is the carnal mind trying to understand the hidden things of God from the human perspective.

Grace teaches that anything in scripture that calls for us to do what Christ has already done is not a call to 'do', but a call to look to Christ, who has already done. Scripture teaches the church, founded upon grace, how to trust in what Christ has done. The commands of the New Covenant teach us how to receive the fullness of life in the Spirit. The warnings of the New Covenant teach us how to avoid being distracted from Christ so we don't invest our lives into a world that is passing away.

None of these deny scripture, but instead they fulfill it. Grace teaches us how to apply the truth of God by faith instead of human effort. Whether it's a call of obedience, or a warning of the temptation of the flesh, grace teaches us to apply these by faith. Not human effort, but by trusting in the transforming power of God's Spirit within us.

Let me conclude this chapter by reiterating this truth. This is of vital importance. When the word is teaching how to walk in life and peace, we understand how to apply that through the spirit. All scriptures point to what God has done, is doing, or what revealed our inability to transform the flesh into a spiritual nature. Scripture teaches how to walk in what God has done, and how to avoid departing from the grace of God to pursue the death of the flesh. New Covenant teaching explains how to walk in what God has done, and how to avoid returning into a life that trusts in the condemnation of the flesh.

Myth – Grace Teaches Christians to Live Unrepentant Lives

The concept of perpetual repentance is not a biblical doctrine, and this chapter will discuss scriptures which clearly refute this belief system. Let's first look at the objection leveled against the doctrine of complete forgiveness through Christ.

The claim is that 1 John 1:9, the only passage in scripture that can be used to support the doctrine of perpetual repentance, was written to the Christian and not to the unbelieving Gnostics. As one critic of complete forgiveness put it:

> "Gnosticism was not yet present during this era of church history. 1 John 2:9 says, 'They went out from among us because they were not of us.' So there were no heretics in the church when John's epistle was written. 1 John 1:9 is necessary because grace is transactional. Until we do our part of repentance, we cannot receive God's forgiveness."

Let's first look at why these claims are false, and then look at what the Bible says about perpetual repentance. The idea that there were no heretics in the church during the era of the Apostle John's letter is hard to fathom. Every epistle addresses heresy to some degree. That is the main purpose of the epistles (or letters to the churches). Nearly every epistle addresses false teaching while also presenting the correct teaching.

There are three known epistles of John. Read his third epistle. He writes to a believer in a church where a false teacher rose up, expelled anyone who didn't agree with him, and forbade anyone for even communicating with the apostles or other Christians outside of his church. This is clearly a false teacher spreading heresy, and since John wrote about it, I think it's a safe assumption to say that heretics were still in the church during John's era. 1 John 2:9 is talking about people who left Christianity because they loved the world. As previously stated, heresy and false teaching is addressed in most epistles, including 1 John 1. This is easy to prove.

To claim that Gnosticism wasn't around in the early church is a misinformed statement. Historically, we know that Gnosticism has existed since at least the time of the Persian Empire. Like many pagan religions, Gnosticism changes with the culture and adopts ideas from other belief systems. Scholars believe the book of 1 John was written between 65 and 95 AD. Around 65 AD a new form of Gnosticism emerged in the areas where the church was prevalent. It was called Gnostic Docetism. Gnostic Docetism believed the following about Christ:

Jesus' body was an illusion

Jesus did not exist in a physical body

Jesus did not die bodily

Jesus did not rise bodily from the dead

All physical manifestations were evil.

Anyone who achieved gnosis (spiritual knowledge) was sinless.

Sin could only exist in the physical world, but their minds were immune from sin because of their acquisition of secret knowledge.

Now I want you to look at two verses in 1 John and see if you can identify the target audiences of each chapter.

1 John 1:1

That which was from the beginning, which we have heard, which we have seen with our eyes, which we have looked upon, and our hands have handled, concerning the Word of life—

1 John 2:1

My little children, these things I write to you, so that you may not sin. And if anyone sins, we have an Advocate with the Father, Jesus Christ the righteous.

In the beginning of this epistle, John goes immediately into defending who Christ is. Let's consider the argument John presents in 1 John 1:

- We have seen Him (Christ) with our eyes.
- Our hands have handled Him.
- The Word of Life was made manifest, and we have seen and bear witness of Him.
- He was with the Father, and then made manifest to us.
- That which we have seen, we declare to you that you may also have fellowship with us.
- God is light and in Him is no darkness.
- If we say we have no sin, we lie.
- If we confess our sins, he is faithful to forgive.
- If we say we have not sinned, we make Him into a liar.

Do you see any rebuttals to the beliefs of Docetism? Docetists taught Jesus didn't exist in a physical form. John skips all introductions and jumps right into the argument against this – we saw Him with our eyes. We touched Him with our hands. This was no illusion, but was the Son who existed with the Father, who was then manifested bodily to us.

Docetism taught that anything physical was evil and of darkness. John argues that in Him there is no darkness, but He is light and sent to take away darkness. Docetism taught that they were sinless because they were living through the knowledge of the mind, and not affected by the sins of the body or a physical world. Because of gnosis, they were sinless. To that John says, "If we say we have no sin, we make Him into a liar."

After presenting his own testimony of experiencing life with Christ in person, and testifying to the glory of Christ, John then presents the true plan of salvation. It is not gnosis (or secret knowledge) that perfects a person, but first acknowledging your sins and recognizing your need of redemption, and then confessing and forsaking a life of darkness – that which is outside of Christ.

Chapter two begins with, "My little children." Chapter 1 says, "That you may also have fellowship with us," clearly indicating that he is addressing people who were not yet in the body of Christ – the church.

Let's dig deeper. Look at the difference in how sin is addressed in chapter 1 and chapter 2. To the unbelieving Gnostics he says:

1 John 1:9 If we confess our sins, He is faithful and just to forgive us *our* sins and to cleanse us from all unrighteousness.

To the children of God he says:

1 John 2:1 My little children, these things I write to you, so that you may not sin. And if anyone sins, we have an Advocate with the Father, Jesus Christ the righteous.

Do you see the difference? Those needing the gospel have the message, confess and forsake and you will receive forgiveness. To the children of God he says, "If anyone sins, we have an Advocate with the Father, Jesus Christ." He is our righteousness, and we confess His righteousness, not our sins. We are under the promise, but those in chapter 1 are not. If we sin, Jesus Christ is our Advocate, or the one who pleads our cause before a judge. And what is our cause? We indeed have sinned when we are drawn back into the flesh, but our Advocate stands in our place to declare us righteous because of His sacrifice.

In a later chapter we'll discuss the consequences for sin, but at this time I want you to focus on the message. The goal, according to the beginning of chapter 2, is that we not sin, but if we do, and everyone does at times, we are not called into fear, but faith. Let's pull in another passage from this book of the Bible, **1 John 4:16-19**

16 And we have known and believed the love that God has for us. God is love, and he who abides in love abides in God, and God in him.

17 Love has been perfected among us in this: that we may have boldness in the day of judgment; because as He is, so are we in this world.

18 There is no fear in love; but perfect love casts out fear, because fear involves torment. But he who fears has not

been made perfect in love.

19 We love Him because He first loved us.

If you still are not convinced about Christ's complete forgiveness, read the above passage again. We are called to believe in the love God has for us, and abandon all fear – including the fear of judgment. What do most people think about when they look at their sin? God is angry. God will judge them. God will withdraw His mercies and blessings. These are all fear-based. Most repentance messages are fear based. Yet the Bible clearly teaches that those who believe in the love of God – which is expressed through grace – no longer have fear.

If you fear, you are not yet perfected in God's love. Faith will then be shifted from the work of Christ to the work of your repentance. Since you can never be certain that you have done everything right, there will never be a time when your righteous acts will alleviate all fear. However, those who fully trust in Christ can rest in confidence knowing that judgment has been removed and we are always acceptable to God.

The concept of 'transactional grace' or 'transactional forgiveness' is not supportable by scripture. Only 1 John 1:9 can be twisted into this belief system. Nearly every book of the New Testament deals with sin, yet not one place are we told that forgiveness is transactional. Each time sin is addressed, the Bible is teaching to remember who you are in Christ, what Christ has done, the promise we have, and the Bible even warns us not to be like Esau who traded away His blessing for a moment of pleasure. The focus is on what we are trading away and the fellowship we are depriving from ourselves. Never are we told that our failure nullifies the work of Christ.

You were never righteous because of what you have done. By faith in what Christ has done, God has credited you with His own righteousness, but never are you presenting your own righteousness to God. If your sinful nature could not negate the work of God before you received righteousness, how can a sin negate the gift of your new nature in Christ now?

Myth – Grace Teaches Unrepentance

If I'm perpetually trying to repair my relationship with God, how can I experience the deeper things of God? How can I experience true fellowship with God? Looking at your sin only keeps your eyes on the flesh. Trying to make a transaction with God for forgiveness only puts the focus on making yourself acceptable to God, which is disbelief in what Christ has already done.

Even the very concept of forgiveness being dependent upon my continual confession of sin is outside the realm of possibility. According to the Bible, to know to do good, and to not do it is a sin.[32] So to omit doing good all the time is sin. Also, to even think evil is a sin. We looked at this earlier when Jesus said lustful thoughts are equal to adultery, and feelings of hatred equals murder. Have you ever spoken evil of a politician? According to Romans 13, this is a sin. To covet, or desire something you don't have is equal to idolatry, which is a sin.[33] The Bible even goes so far as to warn that anything not by faith is a sin.[34]

If perpetual repentance is required for forgiveness, this puts us into a serious predicament. To omit doing the right thing all the time is sin. To do what is wrong is a sin. To think a bad thought is a sin. To desire something God has not provided is a sin. To fail to act, think, and walk by faith 100% of the time in every situation is a sin.

If grace is only transactional, then you are required to confess every sin in every form. How many sins have you forgotten? How many failures of faith have you committed and are not even aware of? Some may say, God is merciful when we forget, but you can't have it both ways. Either every sin has to be confessed, or the confessional ideology is flawed. Keep in mind that the Bible says that if we offend in one point, we are guilty of all the law.[35]

To try to shape the law into something that fits within our abilities is a false assumption. That's what the Jews were doing and why Jesus pointed out how they believed they were keeping the

---

[32] James 4:17
[33] Colossians 3:5
[34] Romans 14:23
[35] James 2:10

law, but the very thoughts of their hearts stood in condemnation of them.

You can't have it both ways. You can't have a law based on human ability. You can't say that God requires confession as long as we can remember our sins. Either God requires confession for every sin, or God has provided a better way. These two cannot be mixed. The law condemns failure. It cannot be shaped into a human standard where we can create our own success.

The Christian is never told that grace or forgiveness is transactional – or dependent upon us doing our part. The Bible does teach and repeat the truth that grace and forgiveness is dependent upon Christ alone, and our only role is to receive this free gift by faith. The Bible also rebukes the idea of perpetual repentance. Look at **Hebrews 6:1**

> Therefore leaving the principles of the doctrine of Christ, let us go on unto perfection; not laying again the foundation of repentance from dead works, and of faith toward God,

Leave behind the concept of laying *again* the foundation of repentance, and begin focusing on faith toward God. Do you see the truth of repentance? The person stuck in the mindset of perpetual repentance never goes on to perfection because they keep re-laying the foundation of repentance from dead works. They are constantly focusing on sin, so they are stuck in the constant process of trying to gain God's acceptance – an acceptance that God has said He has already given through Christ.

A Christian should mature beyond this mindset and grow into a deeper faith and begin trusting in the love God has for them. There should be a point where we begin believing God's promise that we have an Advocate. He has us covered so we can focus on our life in the Spirit instead of the dead works of the flesh we are leaving behind.

Some will argue that the Bible teaches repentance in many places in the New Testament. While this is true, it is not true in the way most churches teach it. The word 'repentance' literally means: to change the mind, or to make a 180 degree turn.

Myth – Grace Teaches Unrepentance

In the true meaning of the word, repentance is very much a part of the Christian's life. When I sin, I recognize I am in the flesh, so I put my mind on the Spirit. Here is true repentance in the Christian life. **Ephesians 4:21-24**

> [21] if indeed you have heard Him and have been taught by Him, as the truth is in Jesus:
> [22] that you put off, concerning your former conduct, the old man which grows corrupt according to the deceitful lusts,
> [23] and be renewed in the spirit of your mind,
> [24] and that you put on the new man which was created according to God, in true righteousness and holiness.

Does putting off our fleshly conduct and putting on the new man of the Spirit sound like a license to sin? Does renewing your mind in the Spirit sound like justification to continue in sin? Quite the opposite, and you aren't even told to wallow in guilt or focus on your sin.

How can we not get excited when we see what we have? Repentance is to realize we have stepped into the dead works of the flesh, and to then put off those things as we put on the new man — that which is a new creation, born of God. Where is confession of sins? Repentance includes renewing our minds by discovering the truth of Christ. His completed work renews our minds and as we put our eyes and minds on the things of the Spirit, we are abandoning the flesh. Renewal, not the confession of the flesh. We don't confess our sins, we confess Christ! Our eyes aren't focused on the deeds of the flesh, but on the works of Christ.

Look at the promise. We are putting on the new life God has given us — a life that is already created in righteousness and true holiness. You are not trying to make yourself holy or righteous. You are putting on the new life God has given you which already has these things.

Stop looking at your flesh and sins. Look to Christ and new life in the Spirit. Trust in what God has already given you. Believe. Stop being faithless and self-dependent and begin walking by faith in God's promises.

Myth – Grace Teaches Unrepentance

Your own holiness couldn't make you right with God before, and it surely can't do so now. Your righteousness was worthless, but the righteousness of God in Christ is priceless. Repentance is to change your mind from the flesh to the Spirit. Let's close this chapter with one last passage from **Romans 8:4-8**

 4 That the righteousness of the law might be fulfilled in us, who walk not after the flesh, but after the Spirit.

 5 For they that are after the flesh do mind the things of the flesh; but they that are after the Spirit the things of the Spirit.

 6 For to be carnally minded *is* death; but to be spiritually minded *is* life and peace.

 7 Because the carnal mind *is* enmity against God: for it is not subject to the law of God, neither indeed can be.

 8 So then they that are in the flesh cannot please God.

Take special heed of verse 8. If you are in the flesh, you cannot please God. This is true even if your flesh is doing religious things. Things like presenting the works of your confession to God as a merit for forgiveness and grace. Every gift of God is by faith in the love God has for us, not faith in what we have done for God. 'Doing your part' is not faith. Trusting in the completed work of Christ is faith.

The Bible clearly teaches that the blood of Jesus' atonement was applied once and for all to the altar in heaven. It can never be reapplied. I won't go into this here since I write extensively about this in the book, 'It is Finished'.

Consider the message of repentance given here. I realize we have used this passage in an earlier chapter, but it also beautifully illustrates the truth we are discussing here. The call of repentance is not to present our sins to God in an attempt to obtain forgiveness. Forgiveness was granted at the cross. Repentance is to change the mind. We blow it when we are in the flesh. We experience life and peace when we set our minds on the things of the Spirit.

Even if we do good works and religious activities, if it is of the flesh, we are no more spiritual than when we are in sin. Or should I say the things we consider to be sin. Pride is a sin. Self-righteousness is a sin. Self-righteousness does not only mean to be haughty and to look down on others. It is to think we are making ourselves righteous by what we do. To try to present our righteousness as independent of the righteousness of Christ is just as much an act of rebellion as blatant sin against God.

In the flesh, you cannot please God. This is just as true for righteous acts as it is for lustful acts. In the Spirit, you have all things that have been given by God. You need not offer a transaction to God in order to obtain, for you have been given all things that pertain to life and godliness.[36]

If you are in the Spirit, you are in life. What more do you think you need to do? By faith, you have already entered into Christ's works and are in a spiritual man that has already been forgiven. If the Bible says our inner man is incorruptible, then all we need to do is walk according to that incorruptible nature. The new man does not need to plead for forgiveness. His life is already in Christ and has been declared as perfected in Him.

As the Apostle Paul said, in the flesh, I serve the law of sin, but in my mind of the Spirit, I serve the law of righteousness. The answer to experiencing a life of righteousness is not to enter into the Gnostic confession, but to confess your faith in Christ and to set your mind on the things of the Spirit. And this is an act of faith. I believe and receive. I trust in the Spirit, therefore I walk in the Spirit.

If I am minding the things of the flesh – including setting my mind on my sins – I am returning under the bondage of the flesh. Then I cannot please God – no matter how many times I confess my sins.

When someone disbelieves, then they will turn to a human effort based religion, but we have been given life and peace in the Spirit.

---

[36] 2 Peter 1:3

Conviction or Acquittal?

Now that we have looked at the only passage in scripture that falsely supports the idea of perpetual repentance and confession, let's look at another passage that is also used to return Christians to bondage. As was the case with 1 John 1:9, this passage only supports the misconception of perpetual repentance when it's taken out of context. **John 16:7-8**

> 7 "Nevertheless I tell you the truth. It is to your advantage that I go away; for if I do not go away, the Helper will not come to you; but if I depart, I will send Him to you.
>
> 8 "And when He has come, He will convict the world of sin, and of righteousness, and of judgment

Even a cursory reading of this passage should be clear, but because Christians are stuck in the mindset of redeeming the flesh, it's easy to start superimposing our assumptions upon the text.

Many will say, "This passage teaches that the Holy Spirit convicts us of sin." Are we the world? Right before this teaching on the Holy Spirit, Jesus said, "You are not of the world, but I have called you out of the world."[37]

The only reason this passage is confusing is because we are interpreting it through human ideas instead of viewing it in the context of the rest of the scripture. What's more is that Jesus interprets this for us. You don't have to guess what Jesus meant, for if you keep reading, He tells you the meaning of this. Look at **John 16:9-13**

> 9 "of sin, because they do not believe in Me;
>
> 10 "of righteousness, because I go to My Father and you see Me no more;
>
> 11 "of judgment, because the ruler of this world is judged.
>
> 12 "I still have many things to say to you, but you cannot bear *them* now.

---

[37] John 15:9

^{13} "However, when He, the Spirit of truth, has come, He will guide you into all truth; for He will not speak on His own *authority*, but whatever He hears He will speak; and He will tell you things to come.

Jesus makes it clear that the Holy Spirit reveals the truth in a threefold way. He convicts the world of sin, the believer of righteousness, and the spiritual principalities of judgment. Each element we must face is covered by the work of the Holy Spirit.

Look at Jesus' words. The Spirit convicts the world of sin, "Because they do not believe in Me." Is this the Christian? There isn't any way to impose this upon Christians for we are no longer called the world, and it cannot be said of the church, "Because they do not believe in Me." We are only in God's family because we DO believe in Christ. The conviction of sin is clearly directed to the unbelieving world.

What's more, let's consider the word conviction. To convict is to find someone guilty. It's to try someone for their crime and the evidence proves that they are guilty. Once someone is found guilty, they are convicted – they become a convict. It's a declaration of condemnation under the law.

This is not the church or the individual Christian. According to scripture, there is no more condemnation to those who are in Christ.[38] The Bible tells us that we are justified through the blood of Christ and we have been found not guilty because of Him. He was declared guilty in our place, and we are found righteous in Him. He redeemed us from the curse of the law, and a Christian cannot be cursed. The curse ended in Christ. According to Jesus' own words, the conviction of sin is to the world that does not believe in Him.

Let's move on. The believer is indeed mentioned in this passage. We fall under the Spirit's conviction of righteousness. The Holy Spirit is constantly revealing to us the righteousness of Christ and our righteousness in Christ. If you want to use the word conviction, it must be in this sense, "The Holy Spirit convicts us of

---

[38] Romans 8:1

Conviction or Acquittal? 69

our righteousness." Since there is no way to condemn someone for being righteous, to be guilty of being righteous would be a declaration of innocence.

Jesus said, "Of righteousness because I go to the Father." To understand this better, let's look at **1 John 2:1**

> [1] My little children, these things I write to you, so that you may not sin. And if anyone sins, we have an Advocate with the Father, Jesus Christ the righteous.
>
> [2] And He Himself is the propitiation for our sins, and not for ours only but also for the whole world.

This is the message to the church. If we sin, Jesus is our Advocate. An advocate is a legal defender who pleads his client's case before a judge. The law stands in judgment, but Jesus is our Advocate – and His defense is a slam-dunk win. "Eddie sinned, but I have already paid the penalty of that sin, and there can't be double-jeopardy."

You see, Jesus is both our Advocate and our Propitiation. Propitiation means to stand in the place of judgment for another person. Because Jesus was already judged for your sins, when you blow it a couple of things happen. The Holy Spirit reveals righteousness to you so your sins are in conflict to your new nature. Then your innocence is declared because Jesus pleads your acquittal to the Father because the law has already been satisfied in Him.[39]

Think of the conviction of righteousness in terms of how we deal with our children. When our children do something out of character, we say something like, "You know better than this," or "This isn't who you are. Why are you acting this way?"

All sin is of the flesh and all acts of the flesh are sin. This is why the Bible says, "Whatever is not of faith is sin."[40] Jesus affirmed this truth when He said, "Whatever is born of the flesh is flesh, and whatever is born of the Spirit is spirit."[41] Even your acts of

---

[39] Romans 8:4
[40] Romans 14:23
[41] John 3:6

Conviction or Acquittal?

righteousness done by human effort is outside of faith in Him and is an act of the flesh. It is born out of sinful flesh and is sin. The flesh cannot produce righteousness. See Isaiah 64:6. I keep driving this point home because it's vital to understand it isn't only blatant sins that conflict with Christ. Both self-righteousness and godlessness is equally in conflict with God's Spirit.

Even Christians get stuck in the mindset of the world. The world thinks that if they do enough good things, God will accept them. The average church member thinks they have to do things to make God accept them. The Bible calls our efforts wood, hay, and straw. These will not survive the fire of God's testing and will never pass over into the Spirit or merit rewards. We become righteous through faith in Christ. We live out our righteousness through faith in Christ. We do good works through faith in Christ.

Sin is of the flesh – whether that sin is good or bad in human eyes is irrelevant. When we are drawn into the flesh, the Holy Spirit convicts us of the righteousness of our new nature in Christ. It's as if the Spirit is saying, "Look at you. You're seeking satisfaction through the flesh. You are trying to serve God through the flesh. You are slipping into sin because you are in the flesh. That's not who you are. Look at your nature in Christ. Look at the Author and Finisher of your faith. Look at the promises of God. The flesh isn't who you are. You are a new creation."

When I recognize that my behavior is aligning with the cravings of the flesh and in contradiction to my nature, I can never find rest. The Spirit gives me no rest. You will have no rest. Even if we can deceive ourselves into pretending that indulging in sin is okay, the end result is an internal conflict that makes it impossible to enjoy sin. This is also why people work themselves to despair trying to merit favor with God. The Spirit never affirms their work, and they mistake the conflict with their nature as a demand to do more. This only occurs because Christians don't know how to discern the prompting of the Spirit. Instead they turn to religious demands in an attempt to replace the leading of the Spirit.

When we finally surrender and turn from our pursuit of the flesh, we also realize that our pursuit was just plain dumb. There was no pleasure, and the time I hoped to gratify the flesh was actually spent trying to suppress the conviction of righteousness.

Here is the one overlooked truth of the conviction of our righteousness. Most Christians are taught to 'get busy for God'. When the Spirit begins to convict us of trying to pursue our own righteous acts through the flesh, we are taught to ignore that call. People are encouraged to fight through burn out, do what they are uncomfortable doing, and stay busy and distracted by works of the flesh done in the name of God.

The Spirit convicts them of righteousness. The Spirit says, "You were saved for good works which God prepared beforehand that you should walk in,[42] but you are trying to produce your own works. You are burnt out because I'm not in it. You are wasting your life on human effort and I'm trying to lead you into My works. You are so busy for God that you can't hear My call."

The Spirit convicts us to focus on Christ and His righteousness, but the church praises you for being so busy. And the truth is that we are serving our flesh in its quest to become self-righteous, and we miss the great plan of God.

The Spirit works just as hard to draw us out of false works as it does to draw us out of false satisfaction.

The flesh is the flesh regardless of whether it's works are religious or blatantly lustful. The conviction of righteousness is calling us to look at Christ, who we are in Christ, and to draw all our life and works from His perfect will. Anything else is an act of the flesh.

The final purpose of the Holy Spirit should be self-evident. Jesus said, "Of judgment because the ruler of this world is judged." The first two pertain to humanity, and the final work of the Spirit is to judge the works of spiritual wickedness that lures us away from Christ. Consider this passage from **Colossians 2:13-15**

> [13] And you, being dead in your trespasses and the uncircumcision of your flesh, He has made alive together with Him, having forgiven you all trespasses,
>
> [14] having wiped out the handwriting of requirements that

---

[42] Ephesians 2:10

was against us, which was contrary to us. And He has taken it out of the way, having nailed it to the cross.

^{15} Having disarmed principalities and powers, He made a public spectacle of them, triumphing over them in it.

This scripture explains that even while we still had a sin nature of the flesh, the Spirit of God circumcised us by taking away that old nature, removed all the requirements against us, and defeated all sin on the cross.

It doesn't stop there. The principalities that once had a stronghold on man before Christ has now been disarmed on the cross, and Jesus triumphed over them. Evil tried to shame Jesus on the cross, but He made a public spectacle of them and put all principalities to shame through the cross.

When Satan, the ruler of this world, comes against us, the Spirit condemns him in judgment because of the cross. The Bible says that Satan is our accuser, proclaiming our failures before God night and day.[43] When you blow it, Satan rushes to God and points to your guilt. The Spirit judges Satan as defeated and points him to the cross. Satan may be able to convince religious people to condemn you. He may be able to convince the world to condemn you. But each time he brings your condemnation before God, he is condemned and cast down.

The next time someone tells you that the Holy Spirit convicts you of sin, rejoice in the truth that the Holy Spirit points to your acquittal. Then allow the Spirit to reveal righteousness to you so you can walk in victory and not condemnation.

This is of the utmost importance, for if you begin falling into the mindset of conviction of sin, your eyes are no longer on Christ, but on your flesh. When someone says, "Look at your sin," your attention is drawn to the flesh. How many people live in defeat because they are trying to do better? They are promising God they won't commit that sin again. Then they try to create victory while shunning the victory of Christ that has already been given to them.

---

[43] Revelation 12:10

Conviction or Acquittal?

True conviction is this. Oh, you sinned? Look at Christ. He is your righteousness. Forget those things that are behind and press toward His high calling. The flesh can do nothing but sin, so look to Christ and by faith in Him, walk in the Spirit. Trust in His promise to subdue your sins.[44] Trust in His declaration of your righteousness. Trust in His promise that He will transform you into His likeness as you focus on Him. Trust in His promise that if you abide in Him, you can do nothing but bear fruit to righteousness. Trust in the promise that your goodness comes from partaking of His nature. Trust in the promise that the Spirit will produce the fruit of love, joy, peace, patience, goodness, kindness, self-control, and every spiritual benefit.

Once you quit trying to fix yourself, you will have eyes to see the call of righteousness. Sin is what we produce when we focus on ourselves – whether we think we're doing good or evil. The fruit of righteousness is the natural result of the one who learns to trust fully in His gift of grace.

You've already been acquitted. Stop focusing on sin and start walking in the promise!

---

[44] Micah 7:19

Myth – Grace Teaches There are No Consequences for Sin

Romans 4:7-8
[7] "Blessed *are those* whose lawless deeds are forgiven, And whose sins are covered;
[8] Blessed *is the* man to whom the LORD shall not impute sin."

People, such as myself, who believe this is a literal promise, are accused of teaching there are no consequences to sin. This simply is not true. We just believe the Bible's promise that these consequences are not us being placed back under condemnation, and we don't believe God withdraws His love and acceptance from us.

A while back I believed as most churches teach – that forgiveness for the Christian is conditional, and that our acceptance was based upon our performance. Of course, I didn't call it 'performance', but since I had to perform good works and stay within a performance based standard of righteousness, that is exactly what I believed and was teaching.

I discussed these scriptures with someone whose simple question changed everything. "Do you believe that Jesus paid for all sin 2000 years ago?" Certainly I did. "Do you believe God's promise that our sins will be remembered no more?" Yes again. "Do you believe we are justified by faith in Christ, apart from our works or anything we do?" Of course. The Bible makes this crystal clear. "Then how can forgiveness be conditional? You can't have it both ways. It's either by grace, or by our efforts. It can't be both."

I had never really thought about me trying to have it both ways. It wasn't the questions that haunted me. It was the comment, "You can't have it both ways." In my heart, I knew this was true. But what about sin? How does our sins fit into the picture? How can it be true that my sins are not imputed, and yet the Bible calls me to walk in God's holiness?

For the next several weeks, I studied the scriptures, compared verses, and prayed for God's revelation. I didn't consult books, teachers, or any other resource. I didn't want to be influenced to adopt someone's perspective, but I wanted the scriptures themselves to compel me. A few weeks into my quest, I was meditating on the scriptures and writing out my thoughts. Then the pieces came together and I received a 'wow' moment. I call it my revelation of grace moment.

For my entire life I had looked at grace as one of the doctrines of scripture. It was one of the pillars in my faith, but in a moment of understanding I realized that grace is the foundation everything else is built upon. In order to understand the New Testament truth of faith in Christ, everything had to be viewed as the reception of grace.

Prior to this, I believed that God gave me grace when I did my part. If I was obedient, I would be blessed. If I examined my life and confessed every sin, I would be forgiven. If I walked in righteousness, God would accept me into His fellowship. The problem is that when I blew it, my faith was dependent upon me getting things right. When I didn't do enough good works, my right standing with God was dependent upon me doing more. Everything was about me doing for God. My faith had been reduced to my love for God, and if I loved God enough, I would please Him. I had a self-performance gospel.

There is a problem with this form of Christianity. It's dependent upon me. It's all about me. I said it was about God, but God's role only began after I did my part. I viewed grace as God giving me the ability to perform. God's power was something I took away from God and tried to use in my life. God's love was something I took away from God and tried to introduce into my emotions and works. Christianity was about taking things from God and trying to do.

This seemed right, but this isn't the gospel message. It's all about God's love for us. We love God because He first loved us. The cross is how God proved His love toward us. Read 2 Peter 1:3-11. Read Galatians 5:22-25. The fruit of the Spirit is what the Spirit produces in the life of those who walk in the Spirit. The spiritual attributes of the Christian life are the things we receive when we become partakers of God's divine nature.

I looked at these as things for me to do, but the truth is these are promises I should be receiving. I am adding to my life the things I am receiving from His nature, not creating accomplishments in my own nature.

True faith doesn't end at the cross. The gospel message isn't that Jesus saved me apart from anything I have done on my part, but now I must keep myself righteous by what I do. No, Jesus saved me apart from any works because of my faith in His gift of grace, and nothing changes. I live out my faith by trusting fully in His grace. The same grace that saved me is the same grace that finishes this work.

The Bible says, Jesus is the Author and Finisher of our faith. Yet we have twisted the gospel into Jesus being the Author, and we are the finisher. To believe you are the finisher is to disbelieve in the work of Christ.

Let's bring in a passage from 2 Peter. This passage begins with the promise that we have received all things through Christ, and we are now partakers of God's divine nature. From a position of being a partaker, we add all the spiritual qualities God has given us. Then the Bible makes an interesting statement in **2 Peter 1:8-9**

8 For if these things are yours and abound, *you* will be neither barren nor unfruitful in the knowledge of our Lord Jesus Christ.

9 For he who lacks these things is shortsighted, even to blindness, and has forgotten that he was cleansed from his old sins.

If these things are yours (faith, virtue, knowledge, self-control, perseverance, godliness, philia love, agape love), you cannot be unfruitful. It's a guarantee. Good works is the inevitable result of the fullness of God's promise being received into your life.

No Consequences for Sin   77

You cannot be unfruitful. It is impossible. Do you believe God's word?

Let's continue. Why does our life lack these things? Virtue means 'moral excellence'. It's the desire to exclude sin from our lives. Godliness is the life that reflects God's character. Notice, you don't produce any of these attributes. These are the natural part of our life of faith. We believe in God's grace, so we look to His nature to provide everything we need for a fruitful life. If you continue reading this passage, you'll see that God abundantly rewards us for receiving these things and letting the Spirit do its fruitful work. He does the work. He produces the fruit. He provides every spiritual quality, but we are rewarded as though we have done it. It's the amazing message of grace. God loves sharing His kingdom with His children. God wants you to inherit His Kingdom. God does not demand that you build it.

Look at verse 9. Why does the Christian miss out on this promise? It's because that person is short-sighted and has forgotten that their sins have been purged. Because they have lost sight of the truth that God has removed our sin, they are blinded by the flesh. They are living a short-sighted life. All of God's promises are before them, but they are so caught up in focusing on sin and human works that they cannot see beyond their flesh to the promise.

Not one Christian lacks this promise, yet very few receive it. Is your life fruitful? Do you see all of God's attributes coming alive in your life? Are you leaving behind the rudimentary things of this life and pressing on into His perfection?

If not, you have forgotten that Jesus purged your sins, and as long as you are focused on yourself and your sins, you cannot see the promise of God. This is the promise of grace. Receive all things from God. Forget about sin; it's of the flesh. In the Spirit, the flesh becomes irrelevant. In the flesh, we are blinded to the things of the Spirit. We are putting the veil back over our own eyes when we look at the flesh.

This is what grace teaches.

What about sin. I know most people are still struggling with this burning question. Of course, if you are focused on the Spirit, this is an irrelevant question. However, there are reasons why the Bible warns us about sin. There are many who have forgotten who they are. There are many who have forgotten that Jesus purged their sin – all sin.

These people are drawn into the flesh, and the more you live in the flesh, the more sin gains strongholds in your life. Of course, those strongholds are broken in Christ, but they are empowered when we submit ourselves back into the flesh.[45]

Let's begin answering this question by continuing in our passage from above. Look at **2 Peter 1:10-11**

> [10] Therefore, brethren, be even more diligent to make your call and election sure, for if you do these things you will never stumble;
>
> [11] for so an entrance will be supplied to you abundantly into the everlasting kingdom of our Lord and Savior Jesus Christ.

Some will read this and say, "Aha! See, you do have to do something to get into heaven." Let's take the legalistic glasses off for a moment and let the scriptures interpret this scripture. Set aside your preconceived ideas for a moment and let's approach this as something to learn as if we are a new believer.

The above ends with a continuation of the promise – heaven's gates will be thrown open for you. The inheritance is yours. It's the revelation that God's desire is for you to be abundantly blessed, abundantly satisfied, and abundantly receive of His abundant grace. Look at how many times the Bible uses the word 'abundant'. A quick search came up with 26 times. That doesn't include the times God used abounding, excessive, and other such descriptions. It almost makes me think God is teaching hyper-grace.

Leading up to this promise is the statement, "Make your call and election sure." Don't mistake this for salvation. Your calling is not merely salvation from hell. Don't sell yourself short. You are

---

[45] Romans 6:16

called to become a king and priest before God. Here is God's desire for you. To him who overcomes, I will give:

To eat from the tree of life in the midst of God's paradise – Revelation 2:7

To receive a new name in the Kingdom – Revelation 2:17

He will receive power to rule over the nations – Revelation 2:26-27

He will be given the morning star Revelation 2:28

I (Jesus) will confess Him before the angels – Revelation 3:5

I will make him into a pillar of the temple of God and will write on him My (Jesus) new name – Revelation 3:12

He will sit with me on My throne – Revelation 3:21

He will inherit all things – Revelation 21:7

The promise of the kingdom is to him who overcomes. Keep in mind that 'he' is used in the general sense. It's the same as when the Bible refers to man as in mankind. It applies to all of God's children – both male and female. (See Galatians 3:28.)

Who is 'he' who overcomes? The Bible tells us. Look at **1 John 5:4-5**

⁴ For whatever is born of God overcomes the world. And this is the victory that has overcome the world-- our faith.

⁵ Who is he who overcomes the world, but he who believes that Jesus is the Son of God?

What do we do? We believe. Our faith overcomes the world, because the man or woman of faith is trusting in God and not themselves. They are receivers of God now; therefore, they will be receivers of God in His Kingdom. The opposite is true for those who don't overcome. Let's look at some scriptures that explain this. Begin with **Revelation 3:11**

Behold, I am coming quickly! Hold fast what you have, that no one may take your crown.

Interesting wording. How can someone take a crown that we have not yet received? According to scripture, we have been given all things through Christ. The crown is already yours, but you have the right to sell it for the things of this life. Hold fast to what you have. This is also affirmed in **Colossians 2:8**

> Beware lest anyone cheat you through philosophy and empty deceit, according to the tradition of men, according to the basic principles of the world, and not according to Christ.

Yes, you can be cheated of your reward. You can abandon faith in Christ and pursue traditions, philosophy, deception, and things that are of the principles of the world instead of faith in Christ. Things like investing your life in a career and neglecting the call of God. Things like investing in religion based on human effort instead of trusting in the truth that you have been given all things through Christ. Things like pursuing lusts, sin, and other things that are of this world only.

The book of 1 John puts it this way. All sin comes from the lust of the flesh, the lust of the eyes, and the pride of life. The first two are based on sensuality and greed, the third fits perfectly into both secular culture and religion. "Look what I did for God," is a statement of pride. Establishing your own righteousness is an act of pride. Anything that does not acknowledge the completed work of Christ, but is dependent upon us, is rooted in pride. So even those who try to keep all of God's commands through religious practices can still be pursuing the world.

One of the clearest explanations for forfeiting our inheritance is given in **Hebrews 12:15-17**

> [15] looking carefully lest anyone fall short of the grace of God; lest any root of bitterness springing up cause trouble, and by this many become defiled;
> [16] lest there *be* any fornicator or profane person like Esau, who for one morsel of food sold his birthright.
> [17] For you know that afterward, when he wanted to inherit the blessing, he was rejected, for he found no place for repentance, though he sought it diligently with tears.

The first thing that jumps out from this passage is that Esau is called a fornicator, but his sin had nothing to do with sexual immorality. He sold himself to the cravings of his flesh. If you know the story, Esau came in from a hard day in the field and was famished. His brother had cooked himself a pot of stew, and Esau begged for it. His brother said, "I'll give you this stew if you'll give me your birthright."

"What good is this birthright if I die of starvation," he said. He then forfeited his birthright for a moment in the flesh.

We also have a birthright through our adoption into God's kingdom. We are inheritors of God's kingdom. Like Esau, we are waiting for the day when that will come to fruition. It was a distant hope, so Esau didn't value his inheritance as much as the cravings of the flesh. He forfeited it all for something that was passing away, but would gratify him now.

We are waiting for our inheritance. Like Esau, we can say, "What good will this do me in the future, I need to satisfy my needs now." Esau would not have starved, though he may have suffered for a few hours from his hunger. He would have watched his brother enjoying his pleasure now, and he would have felt cheated because no one shared with him. Yet his short-sightedness persuaded him that the temporary was more valuable than his inheritance. Then he was cheated out of his reward. The Bible says that Esau's decision showed he despised his birthright.

Esau never considered his consequences until the day of blessing came. When he missed the blessing and realized what he had been cheated out of, he pleaded for just one blessing. He wept bitterly, but it was too late to repent (or turn) from his life's decision.

The Bible then calls us to look at this as our example. Does God love us when we sin? Yes. Did Jesus pay the debt for our sin? Yes. Can we choose to live for sin and despise our birthright as Esau did? Certainly. Does Jesus' complete forgiveness mean there are no consequences to sin?

I suppose this depends on how you look at it. Many who claim the name of Christ do not belong to Him. They may claim that grace permits them to sin, but if sin creates no conflict in our heart, it brings into question whether we have a new nature at all. When Paul was presented with the question, "Does abounding grace mean we are free to sin?" His answer was, absolutely not. How can we who have died to sin continue to live in it?[46]

Who can enjoy wallowing among the corpses? If you are alive, how can you enjoy living among the dead? Why would you want to return to a life of sin and death?

When someone loses sight of the abundance of God and Christianity looks like a life of self-denial, rules, and legalism, they may indeed be tempted to pursue the world. Something within them conflicts with their sins and peace flees from them. At first, sin always seems like liberty until the pleasures give way to emptiness and bondage. People can convince themselves that living for their careers is good, even though something within them longs for fulfillment in Christ. So don't assume that just because someone is living a sinful lifestyle they don't have Christ. From the outside we can't tell. A façade of happiness may be the mask covering the pain.

What is important for you to understand is that living for the world in all its forms is an investment in the flesh. There are consequences in both this life and the life to come. God will chastise His children so they don't miss the promise. And if we realize that we are living contrary to faith, God has promised to restore the years the locusts have eaten.

The world consumes our harvest, and if you look at the example of the Old Testament, God sent the locusts into the land for the purpose of driving His people back to the promise. And once they return, God said, "I will restore what the locusts have eaten."

What an amazing God we serve! Our selfishness causes us to abandon God's promises. God doesn't want us to be like Esau, so He chastises us with the world we are pursuing, and life robs us of joy, blessings, and His promises. Then if we recognize His hand and turn back to life in the Spirit, God restores everything we lost by our foolish choices.

---

[46] Romans 6:1-2

Never buy into the lie that it's too late to experience the fullness of God. The Bible says that God delights in mercy, and is abundant in grace. Mercy is when God acquits us of what we deserve for our sins, and grace is the blessings of God we don't deserve.

God wants you to inherit His kingdom. He will do everything short of violating your will to give you the fullness of His grace. Don't let religion rob you. Don't let sin rob you. Don't let philosophy rob you. Don't invest in the flesh – the life that is passing away.

The consequences to sin is God's chastisement as He corrects us back toward the life of faith. The ultimate consequence is to those who sell their inheritance for this world. The consequences are not a revoking of God's grace. God's love is not limited to your performance. If God said He purged your sin, then you have no right to declare as unclean what God has called clean.

The ultimate consequence is the life that never has faith in the completed work of Christ. Those who never learn that they have received all things and are partakers of His nature are missing out on the depth of God's grace. Religious works and human righteousness is short-sighted. We are either partakers of grace, or we are being cheated. Period.

Complete Forgiveness – Total Acceptance

It's vital to understand forgiveness and total acceptance, for it is the foundation we stand upon as we press ahead into maturity in Christ.

One thing I have learned is that when I didn't understand forgiveness, I never had confidence in my relationship with God. When I felt unworthy of God because of my failures, instead of turning to God for strength, I distanced myself from Him out of shame, fear, and guilt. My perception of God's disappointment in my performance hindered my ability to overcome sin. It did not make me less likely to sin.

What happens when a child has done something they are afraid will lead to punishment? Very young children hide. They don't want the parent to find them. Older children hide the evidence, hoping their parents won't find out. Sometimes they suffer needless consequences because a parent doesn't find out until the harm of consequences begins coming to light. Many times the child finds out the parent would have gladly helped them overcome, but out of fearful guilt, they suffered needlessly. When a child understands their parent's total acceptance, they will face their failure and seek help.

We have a High Priest who has lived among people and can identify with our sufferings.[47] Christ not only accepts us, warts and all, but He is our advocate, helper, and deliverer.

Unlike human parents, God not only can identify with our sufferings of life's temptations, but He is perfect in nature and does not lash out with anger or get frustrated. People get frustrated because their expectations are not met, or they can't regain control of situations.

---

[47] Hebrews 2:17, Hebrews 4:14

God has no unrealistic expectations, for He already sees the end of all things, and has seen it from the beginning.[48] God cannot be frustrated, for His purposes are already established into creation. He cannot be disappointed in you, for He knew your actions before you made your mistakes. And He has already built into your path the way of escape and recovery into His perfect will.

And this is where we begin the quest to understand total forgiveness. It is an accomplished fact because God already knew your sins from before creation, and every sin was credited to Christ's account and then paid publicly on the cross at His death.

Keep this one thing in mind, every sin you have committed was paid for on the cross two-thousand years ago. Before you were born, Jesus had already atoned for your sin. Every one of your sins were in the future when Jesus paid the debt of sin. In fact, the Bible says that Jesus atoned for sin (singular) not sins (plural). Look at **Romans 8:3-4**

> [3] For what the Law could not do in that it was weak through the flesh, God *did* by sending His own Son in the likeness of sinful flesh, on account of sin: He condemned sin in the flesh,
> [4] that the righteous requirement of the Law might be fulfilled in us who do not walk according to the flesh but according to the Spirit.

Jesus did not merely die for your sins. He did not only atone for your sins. It was sin as a whole – all rebellion against God – that was dealt with. I have heard this message preached many times, "When you sin, Jesus reapplies the blood when you confess your sins and repent." I have also taught this type of doctrine before I understood the Bible's teaching.

This sounds good only because we have not truly looked at what the scriptures are teaching. God works in our individual lives to bring us into intimate fellowship with Himself, but when it comes to sin, it is not on an individual basis. Sin entered the world, and through sin, death reigned. According to the Bible, death reigned

---

[48] Isaiah 46:9-10

through one person – Adam – but that curse affected all of mankind. Look at **Romans 5:17**

> For if by the one man's offense death reigned through the one, much more those who receive abundance of grace and of the gift of righteousness will reign in life through the One, Jesus Christ.

Death reigned through one, but grace now reigns through one. In Adam all die, much more in Christ shall all be made alive.[49] Those who are in Adam are under sin. Those who are in Christ are under grace. There is no atoning for each individual sin. Sin – singular – is atoned for, and any who are in Christ have escaped Adam's sin and are now under the righteousness of Christ.

In John 8:34 Jesus said that those who commit sin are slaves of sin. In Romans 6, the Bible explains that we were under slavery to sin, and anyone who turns back to sin is submitting back under slavery. But any who submit to Christ are no longer under bondage to sin. Individual sins are acts of submission back into bondage, but we are free in Christ. Nowhere are we instructed that Jesus must again deal with sin because we fail to walk by faith.

Sin was dealt with on the cross, but we receive forgiveness when we put our trust in Christ. Sin as a whole has already been paid through His atoning sacrifice. We commit sins when we trust in something other than God, but all sin has already been defeated through Christ. The sins we have committed as individuals are judged and removed through the defeat of sin where Jesus removed the curse and provided our reconciliation back to God.

People are judged for their sins because they are in Adam. This is why the Bible says that Jesus did not come into the world to condemn the world. Those who believe in Him escape condemnation, but those who don't believe are condemned, not because Jesus condemns them, but because they are already under condemnation.[50]

---

[49] 1 Corinthians 15:22
[50] John 3:18

It's a false statement to say that Jesus must reapply the blood of His sacrifice each time we sin. According to the Bible, this was done once for all. Once. Not daily. Not each time we repent. Once for all. Let's look at a few passages that clarify this. Start with **Romans 6:10-11**

> ¹⁰ For *the death* that He died, He died to sin <u>once for all</u>; but *the life* that He lives, He lives to God.
>
> ¹¹ Likewise you also, reckon yourselves to be dead indeed to sin, but alive to God in Christ Jesus our Lord.

This is easy to understand, for we all know that Jesus only died once. But what people don't understand is that we who are in Christ must reckon, or account, ourselves dead to sin. It's an act of faith. I believe that Jesus died for sin. I believe that I died with Him on the cross and my flesh was put to death in Him. Now I must also believe that I am dead to sin and alive to God in Christ. It's already an accomplished fact, whether I believe it or not. But when I account myself dead to sin and alive in Christ, I am putting my faith in Jesus' work and receiving this truth. I am entering the work of Christ where sin was already defeated on my behalf.

When the flesh draws me back into a worldly way of thinking and I commit sins, I look back to the cross where I was set at liberty from the flesh, sin, and its reigning power over my old life born through Adam. Because I believe, I account. I know I have new life, so I remind myself that sin no longer has dominion over me, and I step away from a fleshly way of thinking and into spiritual mindedness given to me through Christ. Read Romans 8:6-17 for a full explanation.

Let's go a little deeper by looking at the atonement Christ made for sin. First look at **Hebrews 7:25-27**

> ²⁵ Therefore He is also able to save to the uttermost those who come to God through Him, since He always lives to make intercession for them.
>
> ²⁶ For such a High Priest was fitting for us, *who is* holy, harmless, undefiled, separate from sinners, and has become higher than the heavens;

^{27} who does not need daily, as those high priests, to offer up sacrifices, first for His own sins and then for the people's, for this He did <u>once for all</u> when He offered up Himself.

Once again, the Bible reiterates His one-time offering of Himself, but adds another gem. He now saves us to the uttermost since He is always present to make intercession for us, those who have come to God through Him.

The Bible is painting a perfect picture of how earthly ordinances were given to show us the pattern of what Christ would soon perform in heaven. Take special note of the phrase, "Once for all". We'll see this again regarding the applying of the blood of Christ in this passage from **Hebrews 9:11-12**

^{11} But Christ came *as* High Priest of the good things to come, with the greater and more perfect tabernacle not made with hands, that is, not of this creation.

^{12} Not with the blood of goats and calves, but with His own blood He entered the Most Holy Place <u>once for all</u>, having obtained eternal redemption.

In this passage we find the heart of complete (or total) forgiveness. It is a completed work – once for all. Christ entered into the Most Holy Place in heaven, applied the blood of His sacrifice for sin – all sin – once for all. Sin as a whole has now been atoned for, and we are now forgiven of our individual sins by faith in what Jesus has done.

We receive forgiveness when we come to God through Christ. We experience forgiveness when we put our trust in Christ, though the atonement was accomplished before we were even born. Three different passages emphasize the fact that He did this 'once for all'. Why then are we claiming He must keep doing what the Bible says only needs to be done once.

In the Old Testament, the Bible says the people could not receive God's promise because of unbelief, even though the works were finished before the world was even founded.[51] They missed

---

[51] Hebrews 4:2-3

the promise because they didn't believe in God's work. It was already an accomplished fact, but until they had the faith to enter into that promise, it could not be received. In the same way, the sacrifice of Christ is an accomplished fact. All sin has been atoned for. Every person can be under that redemption, but it can only be received by faith.

Every person is already under condemnation through Adam, but look at **John 3:18**

He who believes in Him is not condemned; but he who does not believe is condemned already, because he has not believed in the name of the only begotten Son of God.

Why are people condemned for sin? They are condemned already because they are born into a sin nature inherited from Adam. They merely choose to remain under that condemnation rather than trusting in the completed work of Christ. It is unbelief that causes them to remain under sin.

Just as the Children of Israel remained in the barren desert because they did not believe God, each person in life is given the call of redemption. All are invited into the promise of rest in Christ. Each person either believes and comes to God through Christ, or they disbelieve and remain in the desert of condemnation.

Once someone is in Christ, they are under His redemption. They are now under the atonement for sin that was applied in heaven once for all. There is no second atonement. There is no reapplication of the blood when we sin and repent. Sin, all sin, has been atoned for and is under the blood of Christ – period.

The Bible never speaks of reapplying the blood. Under the Old Testament covenant, the blood was reapplied yearly for the sins of the coming year. It was constantly applied because it served as a yearly reminder of sin and as a foreshadow of Christ's coming atonement. According to the Bible, the blood of the Old Testament sacrifices could never take away sins.[52] It was never intended to take away sin. The sacrifice was to point to Christ, and by faith,

---

[52] Hebrews 10:11

Complete Forgiveness – Total Acceptance

people obeyed the Old Covenant ordinances as they awaited God's redemption.

According to scripture, the Old Testament ordinance of sacrifice covered sin for the new year. Even in this we see the revelation of the New Testament forgiveness. The Old Covenant atonement for sin was not for the sins of the past year, but for the sin of the upcoming year. They were applying the blood to sins that had not yet been committed. It makes sense, for if someone under the Old Covenant died before they could make the atonement, would the people have had confidence in God's forgiveness? In the same way, Christ atoned sin – even though our transgressions were not yet committed.

Unlike the Old Covenant, in Christ sins are not merely covered, but they are taken out of the way. This is explained clearly in a passage we looked at previously – **Colossians 2:13-14**

> [13] And you, being dead in your trespasses and the uncircumcision of your flesh, He has made alive together with Him, having forgiven you all trespasses,
> [14] having wiped out the handwriting of requirements that was against us, which was contrary to us. And He has taken it out of the way, having nailed it to the cross.

Christ is our covering, and sin is no longer in the picture for the child of God. It isn't hidden or set aside. It is gone, never to be remembered. When you say, "Lord, remember when I did this sin?" God says, "What sin? That was crucified with Christ, buried, and is now taken out of the way." So now the real question is, do I believe or disbelieve God's declaration that sin is gone?

For the believer, the past is no more. Once Christ completed the work, the Old Covenant passed away, for there is no longer a need of the shadow once the One it pointed to arrived. At that point it became sin to keep the Old Covenant. To continue to make sacrifices was a denial of Christ.

In the same way, to claim that Jesus' sacrifice needs to be reapplied each time we sin is a denial of the completed work of Christ. It is to say that Jesus' atonement is insufficient without us keeping an ordinance on our part. If sin can only be atoned if I do something, then I am denying the work of Christ. Faith is not acts of work on our part. Faith is putting our trust in what God has already done.

Let me reiterate this again. When the Bible says, "Jesus atoned for sin once for all," to then say, "The blood must be reapplied each time we sin," is a denial of Christ. The great irony is that we are sinning by claiming that something must be done a second time for our sin.

The only thing that can be done on our part is to believe on Christ. Consider the words of Jesus found in two important passages. First look at **John 3:36**

He who believes in the Son has everlasting life; and he who does not believe the Son shall not see life, but the wrath of God abides on him.

Just as we discussed earlier, faith is the only requirement. Even faith is not by human effort, for the Bible says that God deals us a measure of faith, and now He is asking us to receive His promise of salvation by faith. God is asking us to believe with the power He has given to us. So when we disbelieve, it is because we have cast aside the revelation of God given to us. He gives us the power to believe, invites us into the promise, and then rewards us for possessing what God has given. Then the only work is the work of God that we have received. Let's review a passage we read earlier, **John 6:28-29**

28 Then they said to Him, "What shall we do, that we may work the works of God?"

29 Jesus answered and said to them, "This is the work of God, that you believe in Him whom He sent."

What is the work of God according to Jesus? This is the work of God, that you believe in Christ. Nothing changes after we receive redemption. When we sin and blow it, how do we make it right? It's simple. We believe in Christ's work of redemption. The blood has already been applied and we receive God's works by faith.

When legalists came into the church of Galatia and began teaching people 'Jesus plus human effort', Paul rebuked them saying, "Are you so foolish, having begun in the Spirit, do you now think you are being perfected through the flesh?"[53] By faith they received Christ. They fell from grace by looking to something other than Christ.

Judaizes came into the church and claimed that works of the law were acts of faith, but this was a false claim. The Bible rebukes this belief because the work was actually what man was doing to make himself accepted to God instead of trusting in what God has done to make us accepted. The scriptures called them to return their focus to God's grace and again walk by faith.

The same is true today. We receive Christ by faith and find redemption and forgiveness of sin. God has taken sin out of the way by nailing sin to the cross, and we put our trust in His work and receive the gift of salvation. When we sin again, we still walk by faith, only now we should have an understanding of the grace by which we stand. We look back to the cross and by faith reckon ourselves dead to sin and believe God's promise that we are alive in Christ.

We are trusting in what Christ has already done, not trying to get Him to forgive us again. Begging God for forgiveness is to disbelieve in what Christ has already done. Instead of perpetually trying to keep laying the foundation of repentance, we should be trusting in what Christ has done and believing in that promise.

Rather than slinking away in shame when we realize we have sinned and hiding from God, understanding forgiveness gives us the confidence to get up and begin walking by faith again. Instead of cowering from God or wallowing in defeat, the man or woman of faith looks to the amazing work of Christ, thanks God for what has been done for them, and steps back into a life in the Spirit where victory is a guarantee.

A groveler remains in defeat, but a person who trusts in Christ rises up and lives like the person God has created them to be. Contrary to what is commonly taught, the Bible does not teach us

---

[53] Galatians 3:3

to be in a constant state of begging for forgiveness. When we lose sight of the truth of acceptance through Christ, we begin looking for scriptures that can be twisted into a merit system instead of looking at the whole context of scripture, which teaches that grace cannot be earned by works or by merit.

You are already accepted. You are completely forgiven. Trust in Christ's completed work and walk in His victory!

Myth – Grace Stops People from Doing Good Works

A critic of grace teaching said that grace (aka hyper-grace) teaches that we don't need to do good works. Since we are already accepted and we have already been given everything, there is no need for good works. He claimed that grace actually discourages good works.

Critics of grace did get one thing right – we do believe we have been given all things. Works, like all the benefits of grace, are acts of faith. We believe what the Bible teaches. The Bible says that God finished the works before the foundation of the world.[54] We were crucified with Christ before the foundation of the world.[55] The Lamb of God was slain before the foundation of the world.[56] We believe that just as God entered into space and time to reveal the finished work of Christ, God also enters our time to reveal His finished works and calls us to walk in His works,[57] not create our own.

Instead of rewriting what God's grace teaches us about works, I'm going to borrow this chapter from my previous book, *It is Finished*.

Stepping Beyond the Achievement Perspective

I want you to change the way you think about works. Instead of getting stuck in the human way of thinking of works as what you

---

[54] Hebrews 4:3
[55] Ephesians 1:4
[56] Revelation 13:8
[57] Ephesians 2:10

do for God, begin focusing in on the eternal view of works as what God is doing and inviting you to be a part of. The works of God are not dependent upon you. It is God working, and He invites any who will trust in Him to join Him in the eternal work He has done.

It is not that God needs you and I in order to accomplish His will. God desires to raise up godly men and women to share in His work so that they can share in the rewards of the kingdom.

It is not for God's benefit that we pray and do His works. It is for our benefit. God can fulfill His purposes without us, but then who would share in the joys of the kingdom? God didn't need man in order to create the universe. He didn't need our help to fashion the earth. He didn't ask for man's counsel when He built His purposes into the timeline of creation or prepared the works beforehand.

So why does God require mankind's involvement now? It is for no other purpose than for you and I to become partakers of His glory. Your call into good works is an act of God's grace. He calls you to good works because He favors you and wants you to be a part of what He is doing. Good works are not intended for you to earn anything, but for you to join God as a child works alongside their father.

Let me give an illustration. I'm a gardener. My young children want to help Daddy plant in the garden. I don't need them in order to accomplish my work. I invite them to be a part of the work because I want to build that relationship. My younger children do a poor job. When we planted strawberries, they left the roots exposed. They were haphazard in their methods, but they had such joy in being a part of growing what would soon benefit us.

I went behind them and buried the roots, or rescued the plants that were buried too deep. Sometimes I prepared the rows and said, "Put a seed here, here, and here." Sometimes they succeeded, but most of the time they did not. But I made up for what they lacked.

When the fruit and vegetables produced, they helped me pick. They missed most of the beans and picked a few under-ripened tomatoes. I finished what they missed, but they were pleased to be part of what I was doing.

When they sat at the table, they looked at the fruit of their labors and were happy to enjoy what their work had produced. They got the benefit far beyond the value of their labor, but I didn't invite them because I wanted their labor. I invited them because I wanted them to enjoy growing. I knew they would feel special to be part of my garden. I knew they would put the strawberry on their plate and say, "I helped grow this." The food on the table had more value because they were part of its preparation.

This is what good works are all about. God doesn't need your labors. In fact, when you look to yourself as the source of labor, you are missing the heart of good works. It isn't intended to be labor, but fellowship. You have the amazing privilege of being a part of what God is doing. He is preparing His kingdom, and God has invited you to be a part of it.

When you fall short in your abilities, God doesn't look down and scold you. He embraces you as a child and approves of your desire to be a part of what He is doing. Your abilities are not needed. Your lack of ability is not a barrier, for it is God who works in you both to will and to do for His good pleasure (Philippians 2:13).

Looking to yourself misses the entire point. Good works are the pleasure of joining God as He builds His kingdom so you can enjoy both the experience, and have joy in the finished work.

Don't pollute God's works with human effort. Enjoy the fellowship! Good works are an act of God's grace to your benefit. He could fulfill the kingdom without you, but because He favors you, He invites you into His works.

God wants you to inherit the kingdom. He isn't standing afar off, watching men and women form their own ideas and rewarding those who figure out something that pleases Him. No, God is intimately involved in His church, that was purchased by His blood, and born through His Spirit. And His intention is to call you into His kingdom so you can have intimate fellowship with Him and be rewarded as if it were your work.

It is all of God, and even if we stumble through our labors and make mistakes, God is able to complete is work without the need for us to perform perfectly. Our Heavenly Father has no limitations and is able to correct any mistake we make. And we will make many. Most mistakes escape our notice because He steps in and perfects the work.

My early ministry provides a great example of this. When I first began life in ministry I preached a terrible message to a group of recovering addicts. At the time, I didn't recognize my failure, yet God entered into my flawed efforts and performed His eternal purpose. About a dozen people received Christ that day.

As a young preacher, I needed that encouragement. God cared enough for those people to reveal Himself to them even though my message was flawed. His Spirit was not. He cared enough about me to show His power to me in my works, knowing that it would be nearly a decade before I realized it wasn't my message that changed lives.

This is one of the mistakes I can clearly see. How many will I never see? The truth is, it doesn't matter, for it isn't my work that accomplishes God's eternal purposes. My best work can never accomplish anything eternal. The opposite is also true. My most feeble effort, if it is a work of faith in God's power, can accomplish wonders if God enters that work to accomplish His purpose.

When we trust in His works, we will experience His power. When we trust in our works, we limit His power in us. The one who is lifted with pride will be broken - not as punishment, but so we can see what true glory is. God uses failure to drive us into desperation for His power. The one stuck in human thinking will try to find ways around failure by appealing to human nature and searching for 'methods that work'. The one stuck in human nature will become discouraged and give up. Or they will fall back to methods that are limited to the success of the flesh.

The one who recognizes God's hand will see failure as their limitation and will begin looking to The Lord. God delights in using the person who humbles themselves before Him and has faith to trust in His power to accomplish His works. They recognize that what they do for God is temporal and will have no value beyond this life. This person also recognizes God's power to work within them to accomplish what their best efforts cannot. We must learn to understand that we can bring nothing to God. We are dependent upon Him for every spiritual thing and accomplishment. And He is the accomplisher, not us.

According to the Bible, God fully accomplished His works before the world was created. Let's examine a few passages that make this point clear. We'll begin with Hebrews. The Bible compares the Christian life (those who have received God's promise through Christ) with the Old Testament people (those who refused to trust in God's works). We are jumping into the end of this illustration, but look at **Hebrews 4:3**

For we who have believed do enter that rest, as He has said:
"So I swore in My wrath,`They shall not enter My rest,'"
although the works were finished from the foundation of
the world.

I want to focus in on the last part of this verse, "The works were finished from the foundation of the world." The people missed out on the benefit by not entering into God's work – which rests from human effort and trusts in God's divine work. The people were not asked to accomplish anything for God. They were asked to rest from their own labors and walk in God's works – works that were finished before the world was created.

This is beautifully explained in **Ephesians 2:8-10**
8 For by grace you have been saved through faith, and that
not of yourselves; *it is* the gift of God,
9 not of works, lest anyone should boast.
10 For we are His workmanship, created in Christ Jesus for
good works, which God prepared beforehand that we
should walk in them.

Do you grasp the magnitude of this passage? You cannot be saved by works, for your works have no value in the spiritual world that will one day be revealed. The life we see will pass, for it is temporary, and that which is not seen will become visible, for it is eternal.[58] Add to this the teaching of Jesus on works in **John 6:63**

It is the Spirit who gives life; the flesh profits nothing. The words that I speak to you are spirit, and *they* are life.

Anything accomplished by the flesh (human effort) profits nothing. Only the Spirit can produce the things that have life. Your efforts are bound to a temporary world and cannot pass into the eternal world to come. However, God invites you to enter into His eternal work so that you can receive the things that will remain when this life passes away. And God is not asking you to accomplish anything, for there is nothing you can accomplish. There is not any work you can do that can enter into the spiritual life of God's kingdom. You are bound to the physical, but God is not.

Notice the words above. You are created (your new spiritual life in Christ)[59] for the good works that God prepared beforehand. These are the works the Old Testament people missed, for they were focusing on their world instead of God's kingdom. In fact, when they realized they missed the promise, many of them decided to do God's work and take the promise by human effort. These were driven out of the Promised Land and many were destroyed by their enemies.[60]

Human effort cannot accomplish the work of God. Either God is leading us into His works, or we cannot enter. Period. Either we answer God's invitation by faith, or we cannot enter. Period. Faith is always trusting in God's power, revelation, and gifts of His favor. Faith in ourselves is not of the Spirit and cannot put us into God's will. Working without faith is mere human effort.

In Christ, we are a new spiritual creation. As we learn to trust in Christ, we begin to see the path of good works that God calls us to walk in. Take note that the Bible does not tell us to make the good works, but to walk in what God has already made. This is

---

[58] 2 Corinthians 4:18
[59] 2 Corinthians 5:17
[60] Numbers 14:40-45

missed by most Christians because a human-effort gospel is preached in most Christian circles.

Let me provide another illustration from my early church life. As a youth, my church began teaching on giving. They held up the testimony of a man who felt that God was calling him to give ninety-percent of his income to the Lord. He obeyed and God greatly blessed him. "Do you see what God did for this man?" the preacher said, "This is what God will do for you. You must give until it hurts."

Let me say first that I indeed believe that God called that man to give. God blessed because this man trusted in God's call. In the opposite way we see an example of God's power through the orphanage ministry of George Muller. His ministry was not on giving, but receiving. Muller felt called by God to completely trust in God's provision without having to ask for donations. He believed that God was leading him to trust, not beg. He had many struggles and times when he didn't know how he was going to pay the bills or buy food, but he saw the miraculous work of God in many unexpected ways. Muller stands as a testimony that God's call is trustworthy, even when circumstances would indicate otherwise.

History is sprinkled with people who abandoned all to trust the Lord. It's interesting to note that God rarely asks each person to trust in the same way. Some leave lucrative jobs and go into missions. Some keep lucrative jobs and give money. Some are everyday people trusting God to accomplish eternal things in their simple lives.

Jesus asked the rich young ruler to sell all he had and give to the poor, but He never asked such things from others. Jesus saw Matthew at the receipt of customs and said, "Follow me." Matthew left his life and job behind and followed Jesus. Yet when Jesus rescued the demon possessed man, He commanded him to stay. The once insane man stood in his right mind. Instead of praising Christ, the people asked Jesus to leave their coasts because they were afraid. The cured man begged to follow Jesus, but Jesus would not permit him to come, but said, "Go and tell your friends and family what God has done and the compassion He has had on you."[61]

Do you see that God's work in one person's life is not the call of God in the life of another? Who was called by God to accomplish His will? Matthew or the man set free from demonic possession? Both. One's calling was to leave all and follow. The other was called to stay and be a testimony to his friends and family. Neither man could adopt a different calling and stay in God's will.

To go when God calls you to stay is disobedience that cannot be blessed. To stay when the call is to go is disobedience that cannot be blessed.

It's important to learn to follow God's call for you and not His call for others. A great testimony should not be mistaken as a call for action on your part. It should inspire us to trust the Lord, but God determines the call. People who put God to the test without His calling will fall short, for they are serving God by human effort. Those who hear the call and refuse to trust, miss the glory of God that would have been revealed. Those who try to imitate someone else's call are equally in disobedience and should not expect God to bless. They will have turned faith into legalism, for human effort and man-made regulations have displaced the prompting of the Spirit.

To illustrate this, let's go back to the example from my youth. "Give until it hurts," was the message. In fact, I hear this echoed frequently from teachers and preachers; however, this cannot be found in the Bible. Abraham had great wealth, but did not give until it hurt. David had great wealth, and though he set aside gold and silver for the future temple, he also did not give until it hurt. The Apostle Paul did. He gave up everything for the sake of Christ. Yet the Bible does not point to Paul as any higher example of faith than Abraham or David. David is called the man after God's heart. Abraham is called the friend of God and the father of faith.

Abraham trusted God by receiving. The Apostle Paul trusted God by leaving everything behind. Both were obedient in their call. If Abraham had refused to receive, he would not have been living

---

[61] Mark 5:1-19

Myth – No Good Works

by faith. If Paul had focused on receiving, he would not have been living by faith. It is God who reveals His call and we who submit to His will. The focus is not on our works, but trusting in God's work. We must let go of what we think the call should be and trust in what God reveals to us. Anything else becomes a work of the flesh – regardless of what we sacrifice or what we accomplish in this life.

God may speak to your heart when you hear a testimony, and you may indeed feel the prompting to enter the same call. Yet I have met many Christians who are creating a false calling by an emotional compulsion or feelings of guilt. When we see the amazing work of God, the tempter may throw guilt upon you and say, "Why aren't you doing that?" Yet God doesn't measure faithfulness by accomplishments but by obedience by faith. Remember, someone had to be the tent peg holder for the Tabernacle of Testimony in the wilderness. Not everyone is called to be a Moses or Aaron. What's more, is that God rewards us for faith in His call. No one is rewarded based on their fame, recognition, or accomplishments. The work is God's and we are all part of the body of Christ. Each member's role is vital to the whole body.

I fell into this trap in my youth. Because of my ignorance of the word of God, I believed that I should give until it hurt. However, when works are by human effort and not by the call of God, we become the ones who determine what is good works and what is not. And our perspective is flawed.

If I believe I make God proud when I do enough good works, then doesn't that mean I feel I've disappointed God if I don't do enough? And what is enough? In my case, I doubled my tithe. But it didn't hurt, for I could still afford to go to the movies. I upped my giving, but it still didn't hurt. I could still afford to go to a hamburger stand. I upped it more, but I still could afford gas for my car. How much would it take to hurt? How much sacrifice is enough? I was still living at home back then, so I knew I would not starve, even if I gave all my money away.

People praised me for 'being a giver'. I was accounted as spiritual by those in the church, but I felt like I was in bondage. I could not do enough to please God. It was as 1 Corinthians 13 states, "Even if I give my body to be burned as an offering, if I lack love (agape), it profits me nothing."

Wait a minute! Does that mean I can sacrifice everything, including my own life, for the sake of Christ and it means nothing? If I give until it hurts, it might still mean nothing? Yes, that is exactly what this means. I am not called to kill myself for God's kingdom. I am called to rest in the agape love of Christ, cease from my own labors, and walk in the works God has prepared for me to walk in.

If God calls me to give ninety percent, I can walk confidently because it is all His work and not my own. If I am called to leave my home behind and become a missionary, I can rest in Christ while I walk in His works to do ministry. If I am called to stay where I am and just influence my peers at work and live out my faith as a ministry to those around me, then I can rest and be confident in God's calling – regardless of what others are doing or telling me I should do. God has made the path of our works and He alone issues the call. Anything else is wasted labor by human effort. Any work, even that which is an offering to Christ, but is not God's move in my life, profits nothing.

Don't forget what Jesus explained in Matthew 7:22-23. Jesus tells about many who will present their good works to Him at the end of this life. They present many good deeds that they have done in Jesus' name. These works are things we all would acknowledge as good. Healing, feeding the poor, teaching the word of God, etc. These were done by well-intentioned people who served in the name of Jesus, but Jesus says, "Depart from Me, you are a worker of lawlessness. I never knew you."

How can good deeds done in Jesus name be a work of lawlessness? This completely dismantles the belief system of most Christians. The truth is that they did not seek to know Christ. They did not enter into His works. They sought their own efforts and never sought the righteousness of Christ. Or as the Apostle Paul said, "Seeking to establish their own righteousness, they did not find the righteousness of God."[62]

---

[62] Romans 10:3

Myth – No Good Works

The truth is, God has already done the work. With or without you, His purposes will be accomplished. Or a better way of saying it might be, God has already accomplished His purposes. Let's look at another passage that illustrates this – **1 Peter 1:20-21**

> [20] He indeed was foreordained before the foundation of the world, but was manifest in these last times for you
> [21] who through Him believe in God, who raised Him from the dead and gave Him glory, so that your faith and hope are in God.

The work of Christ is reiterated in Revelation 13:8 when it says, "the Lamb was slain from the foundation of the world." How can God say that Jesus was slain for us before the world was founded? It's a great mystery to the human mind, but a great revelation to those who view life through the eyes of the Spirit. The fact is that God established His works completely, and then formed creation around His completed work. He wove creation into His good works and reveals these to any who will walk by faith. During the timeline of creation, God enters our realm to make His work manifest to those who walk by faith. He then asks us to walk in the works He reveals to us.

This is why Psalm 139:14-18 can say God saw us before we were formed, wrote our life into His book, and put so much thought into our life that it would be easier to number the sands of the sea than to count the number of His good thoughts toward us. Before we had a breath, our life was already written out. Before the earth was formed, Christ had already been slain for us. This was reality before time began, but was not revealed to us until God entered into time and space to reveal that work on the cross.

We are bound by time, but God holds time as an object in His hand. We receive God's works and promises when we trust in His works and not our own.

And here is another great mystery that's hard for people to comprehend but revealed to us by God's Spirit. The works were finished before time began, but we must believe in the works of Christ and enter by faith. We are not automatons. Just as the Old

Testament saints could not receive the promise because they rejected faith, we also must enter by faith or miss the promise. God's works are an accomplished fact, but God has revealed them to us so we can enter by faith and walk in them. Or we can do as many before us – trust in our own works and only inherit the things of this life that are passing away.

Each day, as you seek the Lord, God enters time at the point where you are, invites you to trust Him, and calls you into His works so you can receive the reward of what He has done simply because you trusted enough to walk with Him.

Around you many voices are competing with His call. Temptation promises fulfillment outside of Christ. Jobs call us to devote ourselves beyond what is necessary. The world influences us to invest our lives in stuff and pleasures that are limited to this life only. Religion calls for us to work for God by our will and human effort. People invest their lives in activities that are not the calling of God. Sometimes people hear the call of God, but instead of looking to His works, they believe the false idea that we must do our own works for Him.

God is patient and works with us to reveal the truth of His purpose. Though we may falter, the person who trusts in Him cannot fail. Take to heart the words of **2 Peter 1:8, 10-11**

[8] For if these things are yours and abound, *you* will be neither barren nor unfruitful in the knowledge of our Lord Jesus Christ. [10] Therefore, brethren, be even more diligent to make your call and election sure, for if you do these things you will never stumble; [11] for so an entrance will be supplied to you abundantly into the everlasting kingdom of our Lord and Savior Jesus Christ.

Do you see the wonderful promises of this word? If these things are yours and abound in your life, you cannot be unfruitful. You cannot fail. You will never stumble. The gates of heaven will be thrown wide open to receive you. Isn't this an amazing promise?

The only thing required of you is to be diligent to make sure you follow the call and to receive from God so you abound in God's works. And this goes back to what we discussed in the first chapter

– His divine power has given you *all* things pertaining to life and godliness. These things are already yours. Be diligent to not allow yourself to be drawn away from the surety of God's call. Be diligent to make sure you are not seeking your own works. Be diligent to receive all things He has given you.

When you are abounding in Christ, you have all things and the gates of heaven eagerly await to receive you. What a promise! This is the true message of works. Trust in God's works. Walk in what He has accomplished and is inviting you into. Don't allow yourself to come short in any gift. Do not allow yourself to be distracted from Christ.

The promise is yours. Abound in it.

Sanctification

The misconception of sanctification prevails throughout much of modern church thought. This is in spite of the fact that the Bible addresses this clearly. The concept of sanctification is addressed more than thirty times in the New Testament.

Let's look at how sanctification is taught in most Christian circles. It's said that Jesus saves us, and we must now work to become sanctified. We have to align our lives and behavior with Christ's so we can be sanctified. Justification is given at the cross, but sanctification is the process of learning how to become like Christ.

The word 'sanctification' means to be purified, consecrated, and set apart for God.

Let me ask you a question. Can a polluted lake purify itself? Can a corrupt soul choose to become clean? Can I decide to make myself set apart for God? People try to do this all the time. Life and history is filled with people who tried to make themselves righteous and make themselves into 'God's man'. They do so by establishing a legalistic system that fits their own nature, and then declare themselves holy by a standard they have established.

This cannot work. God said we must be holy as He is holy. We can't keep the law only in the areas that fit our culture and lifestyle. A good example of this is the modern day Sabbath keepers. Some go as far as to say that we are under condemnation if we don't worship God on Saturday (which is the Sabbath) because one of the Ten Commandments is to keep the Sabbath holy.

While there is nothing wrong with choosing to worship on Saturday, they are not keeping the Sabbath. The law of the Sabbath is not merely a command to worship. The command is to do nothing except rest in your houses. No cleaning, no setting the table, no cooking, no buying, no selling, no commuting. Not only that, your animals can't do anything nor can any strangers with you. If you go to the restaurant, you have broken the Sabbath. If you buy gas or medicine, you have broken the Sabbath. If you pick clothes off your kids floor, you have broken the Sabbath.

Human nature tries to conform the law into ways we can keep it, but just because we can't keep the law doesn't make the law flexible. The law is meant to condemn and drive us to Christ. What's more, Jesus is our Sabbath rest, for we who have entered that rest have ceased from our own labors.[63] Once again we are trying to do in the law what cannot be done by human nature, and we are not trusting in what has already been done.

Sanctification is the same way. It's man attempting to make himself feel righteous by what he does. Yet man can never sanctify himself. Sanctification is the work of God; not the work of man. Let's look at a few passages that help clarify this. Begin with **1 Corinthians 1:2-3**

> [2] To the church of God which is at Corinth, to those who are sanctified in Christ Jesus, called *to be* saints, with all who in every place call on the name of Jesus Christ our Lord, both theirs and ours:
> [3] Grace to you and peace from God our Father and the Lord Jesus Christ.

Here is an interesting introduction. The Apostle Paul is writing to the church of Corinth, and he calls them sanctified in Christ Jesus. If you are familiar with this book of the Bible, you know Paul is about to scold them for many un-Christ-like behaviors. He rebukes them for being fleshly minded, divisive, selfish, sexually immoral, and several other errors in their behaviors. Yet he begins with the words, "To those who are sanctified in Christ Jesus."

If you look at how Paul guided this carnally minded group of believers, he is constantly reminding them of who they are in Christ and what they have been given in Christ. He does not tell them what they should do for God. Nor does he tell them to grovel in guilt and ask God to re-forgive them. His argument is, "This is who you are. Stop being distracted by what you were." Consider **1 Corinthians 6:11**

---

[63] Hebrews 4:10

And such were some of you. But you were washed, but you were sanctified, but you were justified in the name of the Lord Jesus and by the Spirit of our God.

If you read the preceding verses, Paul is going down the lists of sin in the culture around them. Then he concludes by saying, "Such were some of you, … but you are sanctified." He goes through the work of Christ and tells them they were sanctified, justified, and washed. All of these are listed in the past-tense. Not will be or hope to be, but you were made into these things through Christ. The source of their spirituality is clearly explained in **1 Corinthians 1:30-31**

> [30] But of Him you are in Christ Jesus, who became for us wisdom from God-- and righteousness and sanctification and redemption--
> [31] that, as it is written, "He who glories, let him glory in the LORD."

Jesus became for us wisdom, righteousness, sanctification, and redemption. Jesus is our sanctification. We are sanctified because we are in Him. Period.

Verse 31 explains why this is important. Many try to establish their own glory by making themselves righteous, sanctified, and by trying to accomplish various other spiritual achievements. God rejects these. Not one person will ever stand before God and say, "I have sanctified myself for You." Nor will any be permitted to say, "I have made myself righteous and just."

All we have in our life has been given through Christ so that we see the amazing gift of God's love – grace. Our flawed nature can never measure up to God's standard. Even after redemption, we still are incapable of making ourselves perfect. Every person slips into selfishness. Every person serves their own flesh in varying ways. Some of those ways look very good to our human eyes, but they are not even close to God's standard of perfection.

God designed us to be dependent upon Him. That way you and I can recognize the love God has for us. He doesn't love you because you are coming along in the process of sanctification. He doesn't love you because now you can produce righteousness. He doesn't love you because of your good works. God loves you because He is love. Because He loves you, God says, "I have made you sanctified. I have made you holy. I have made you righteous. Trust in My gift of grace to you."

That is when we see the glory of God given to us. We then glory in our sanctification because He has sanctified us in Christ. I rejoice in Christ where I find my gift of righteousness. I then can run to the throne of grace with confidence both when I have need, and when I am enjoying the goodness He is producing.

We are always in need, but sometimes we are distracted from grace and we trust in the flesh. Sometimes we experience so much of God's glory that we forget it's a gift and not our doing.

Your sanctification reveals the power and love of God. Your glory is either in the Lord, or it is a counterfeit faith. Anytime we are trusting in what we do for God, we are trusting in a counterfeit faith.

Before leaving this topic, let's look at a few verses that are misused to teach 'the process of sanctification'. First look at 1 Thessalonians 4:2-4

² for you know what commandments we gave you through the Lord Jesus.
³ For this is the will of God, your sanctification: that you should abstain from sexual immorality;
⁴ that each of you should know how to possess his own vessel in sanctification and honor,

So is this passage teaching that it's God's will that we sanctify ourselves? Quite the opposite. God's commands in the New Covenant serve two main purposes. Commandments guide us to discover the deeper things of God. For example, the command to study the Bible is given so we explore the truths of God's word. In it, we discover things we could not have found without studying.

The command to be thankful in everything is another good example. When I know I have to be thankful, if I choose to obey this command, it forces me to examine life with spiritual eyes of expectation. Grumbling and complaining puts my focus on myself, my circumstances, and the flesh. Yet the same things that cause me pain or discomfort, if I begin to obey the command to be thankful, forces me to consider these questions, "What is the purpose behind this? What is God doing? Is God using this hardship to teach me something?" Then I begin to discover both God's purposes behind struggles, and the truth that when my fulfillment comes from Christ, circumstances cannot rob me of joy.

Other commands serve as warning signs. To pursue sin is to allow the world to rob me of what has greater value. I am sanctified – set apart by God for God. Do I step outside of a life of sanctification to pursue the sins that can only produce death? Do I forfeit my inheritance for a life that is passing? Without commandments, how do I know when I am stepping outside of faith?

God's commands are warning me – look, this is in contradiction to your life in Me. Returning to the flesh is to abandon the treasures of life in the Spirit. In the passage above, it's the will of God for you to be sanctified. Since we have already seen that we have been sanctified, sexual immorality can only take us out of life in the Spirit. The flesh isn't sanctified, but it's God's will that I live as a sanctified believer. Abstaining is to avoid rejecting God's will of my sanctification to step into the realm of death where sin seeks to rule over me.

This leads us to the next passage that is misused to teach that sanctification is not a gift of God, but is something we must do. Look at **1 Thessalonians 5:23-24**

> 23 Now may the God of peace Himself sanctify you completely; and may your whole spirit, soul, and body be preserved blameless at the coming of our Lord Jesus Christ.
> 24 He who calls you *is* faithful, who also will do *it*.

Aha! Sanctification *is* a process, right? Look carefully through this passage. First notice who does the sanctifying. God Himself does the sanctification. He who calls you...will also do it. What is your role? It is to trust in Him who does the work. You are receiving the work of God, not doing the sanctifying.

The message is the concept of transformation. You are already sanctified in Christ. Your spirit is in Christ, of the Holy Spirit, and is incorruptible. It can't be sanctified because it is already of God, for God, and in God. Yet there is a completeness God is working toward. Your soul falls into temptation. That's where your personality, emotions, and desires reside. I go into the Bible's teaching on the spirit, soul, and body in other books, so I won't cover that here.

What you should understand in the 'process of sanctification' is that you already are sanctified, but as you learn to walk in the Spirit – which is to live by faith in the completed work of Christ – your behavior will begin to conform to your spiritual nature born of God, instead of drawing from the desires of the flesh.

The Bible says that we are transformed into His likeness as we behold Christ. As you and I learn how to trust Christ and abide in Him, God begins to transform our behavior into agreement with the nature we have been given by God. The flesh won't be transformed until we are changed at His coming. That's when the completion occurs. However, as we learn to walk by faith, our behavior begins to draw from our sanctified life instead of the unsanctified flesh.

Remember, it is God who works in you to accomplish His will for His good pleasure.[64] Jesus is the Author and Finisher of our faith.[65] Our command is to look to Him. When we look to Christ and walk by faith, we are walking like the sanctified person God has created us to be in Christ. When we walk according to the flesh, we are walking like the person we have left behind.

Sanctification is not what you do. It is you trusting and walking in what God has done!

---

[64] Philippians 2:13
[65] Hebrews 12:2

The Purpose of Grace

Grace teaches us that the flesh is not our focus. It's not our concern, fear, or hindrance. We have the promise that God has taken care of the flesh so we can put all our focus on walking in the Spirit – the place where all good and all promises are inherited. Even if you blow it, the flesh is not your concern. The more you focus on the flesh, the more you'll walk according to the flesh.

Does this mean we can live anyway we want? Do you realize the Apostle Paul was asked and answered these same questions throughout the book of Romans? His answer was simple. How can we who have died to the flesh continue to live in it? To do so is to forget that we have life.

Certainly people can focus on death. The church is filled with people stuck in this mindset. They focus on death because they are not experiencing life in the Spirit. It's not only 'Those pastors who leave their wives and run off with their secretaries,' as critics of grace claim. It is also those who grovel in failure and wrestle against sin in their own power. It is those who try to make themselves righteous and try to please God by anything other than faith.

People have no problem with this statement of evangelism, "You don't have to do anything to clean up your life. Come to Christ as you are and He will take away your sins and transform your life."

Why then do people a have problem with saying this same thing to Christians – those who know Christ and understand faith. Or at least should understand faith. The truth is that the Christian life is lived the same way it is entered – by faith in Christ.

Stop worrying about your sins. Stop worrying about whether you are measuring up to God. You only have one thing to focus upon – walking by faith in the Son of God. As Paul said, "I press on, forgetting the things that are behind and pressing on toward the high calling of God." That high calling is the call of walking by faith. That is what it means to walk in the Spirit. It is to walk in complete trust in what God has done and is providing.

When you blow it, God isn't calling you to do anything but trust in His provision for sin, and then to step out of the flesh and begin walking by faith. Repentance is to change our minds from the flesh to the Spirit. Repentance as it is taught in most churches is a call to remain focused on the flesh and make right our wrongs. Yet according to the Bible, a good act of the flesh is no better than a bad act of the flesh. What is of the flesh is flesh and is always opposed to the Spirit.

God has your back. He's taken care of the flesh. It may rise up and at times you may be drawn to submit to it. When this happens, grace – true grace – teaches you to forget those things and press on toward the Spirit. Leave your failures in God's hands and trust Him to deal with the flesh. The more you learn to walk in the Spirit, the more the flesh loses its grip on your life.

Do you have an addictive behavior or a habitual sin? Forget these things and press on toward the Spirit. If they rise up again, take your eyes off the sin and your failure in that sin. Press on toward the high calling of God. His Spirit will transform your life out of that sin as you learn to trust in Him. It's not your role to clean up the flesh. It's your role and calling to pursue the Spirit. Then all the strongholds of sin will be forgotten in the past as they are trampled underfoot by God's abundant grace.

The only reason this doesn't work in most Christian's lives is because they don't trust in God's promises. They don't trust grace, so they fall back to the works of the flesh. The flesh packages its rebellion against the righteousness of Christ as self-righteousness, good deeds, and religious efforts. Yet these things are just as harmful as habitual sins. In fact, they are more harmful because religion blinds us to our need. If Satan can't tempt you with lust, he will tempt you with religion. Both sin and self-righteousness take your focus off Christ, so he wins if he can persuade you with either method.

When you sin, the relationship you have with God isn't breeched. The breakdown is never on God's end. It is always we who hide from Him, not God who hides from us. Sin is an act of disbelief in God's goodness. We don't believe God's promise that

He will not withhold good from any who love Him, so we try to fulfill our desires without Him. In the same way, when we don't believe God's promise of forgiveness and acceptance, we fall back to trusting in our religious methods as we try to make ourselves right with Him.

The Bible says that even if we are faithless, God remains faithful, for He cannot deny Himself.[66] You are the temple of God and the Holy Spirit is within you. Because God is within you, you are always in fellowship with Him according to the inner man. When you don't believe God and act out in disbelief, God doesn't withdraw from you. He is always within you. It's not possible to deny Himself, so that fellowship is never broken. Yet we account ourselves unworthy; therefore, we refuse to believe in our position in Christ. Yet our disbelief doesn't change what God has promised. It only prevents us from walking according to that promise.

Grace gives us liberty from the flesh. While those who don't understand grace are wrestling with the flesh, those who trust in grace are free to leave the burden of the flesh behind and pursue the promise of the Spirit without distraction.

When the weakness of the flesh threatens our minds or even causes us to falter, God stands by our side and says, "My grace is sufficient. My strength is made perfect in your weakness."[67] As long as we are trying to fix ourselves, we are standing outside of God's strength. As long as we are trying to overcome our sins and failures, we are missing the promise of God's strength.

Do you struggle with sin? Life controlling issues? A temper? Lusts of the eyes? Name the temptation and the Bible gives you the answer. Stop worrying about sin and start pursuing grace.

The Bible tells us that where sin abounds, grace much more abounds. Much more. It's not an equal force to stop an equal force. The promise is that grace abounds much more than our sin. God's grace overruns sin and drives it back out of our lives.

It's interesting that as these principles are explained in Romans 5 and 6, the Apostle Paul asks a question that he knows

---

[66] 2 Timothy 2:13
[67] 2 Corinthians 12:9

　　　　　　　　　　The Purpose of Grace

will arise in people's hearts. It's the same accusation the religious crowd levies against grace today. "If where sin abounds grace more abundantly abounds, does this mean we can sin that grace may abound?"

Do you see that the same concerns today were the same concerns the Apostles of Jesus faced at the birth of the church. People are saying, "Look at this hyper-grace theology. This is teaching people that sin is okay. If you teach this, you are giving people a license to sin."

People outside of the full assurance of grace are looking at grace from the human perspective. If God is not holding sin against us, then that means we are free to sin at will. Yet the message of grace is that we have died with Christ and have been set free from this body of sin and death. God has rescued us from the flesh and it's strongholds on our lives. Why would we then want to submit back to sin and crawl into the grave filled with corpses and death? That doesn't even make sense. Only those who have never experienced life would think a graveyard was worth the investment of our lives.

The message of grace isn't 'have fun with sin.' The message of grace is that sin, death, and the flesh have no more power over your life. They are irrelevant to the person with new life. A life that abounded in sin can be just as free as the life escaping from petty sin. That is petty sin based on the human view of sin. All people are under condemnation without Christ – regardless of how big or small their sins may appear to be.

You may have addictions, a horrible past, and the baggage of a lifetime of accumulated sin and destructive behaviors. The message of grace is, "So what?" Stop worrying about the sins that cling to your flesh. Pursue your life in the Spirit and let God worry about stripping the flesh of its power.

An addiction may have risen up and has drawn you back into temptation. So what? God's grace is sufficient to overthrow any sin. For a moment it may recapture your mind by persuading you of its power to enslave you, or of its power to gratify your needs. Suddenly you realize you are under the weight of the flesh again.

But then you remember God's promise – sin shall not have dominion over you, for you are no longer under the law, but are under grace.

By faith, you then receive the promise of God's grace, He subdues your flesh, and you can again run this race of life without distraction or the burden of failure. Your weaknesses and sins may be many, but sin cannot abound over grace; grace abounds over sin.

This is not the message the church now preaches. When a person fails, they will hear things like, "Look at your sins. Your fellowship with God has now been broken, and God cannot receive you until you get it right. You must go through the forgiveness transaction. When you get it right, God will again forgive."

A person is then plunged back into a legalistic way of thinking. I must do something in order to make God accept me. I must get rid of this sin so God can receive me. How many times do we promise God, "I'll never do that again?" Or, "I'll try harder. I'll become holy for You." These are promises you cannot deliver. They are promises God doesn't even want from you. Here is what God wants. **Psalm 33:18-22**

> [18] Behold, the eye of the LORD *is* on those who fear Him, On those who hope in His mercy,
> [19] To deliver their soul from death, And to keep them alive in famine.
> [20] Our soul waits for the LORD; He *is* our help and our shield.
> [21] For our heart shall rejoice in Him, Because we have trusted in His holy name.
> [22] Let Your mercy, O LORD, be upon us, Just as we hope in You.

I am going to contradict something I once taught. In the Old Covenant, the fear of the Lord was to fear the consequences of sin. Yet even in the Old Testament, the coming grace was revealed in many ways. This is one of those ways. The fear of God for those who are in His promise is this – to hope in His mercy.

God desires a heart that hopes in His mercy, trusts in His name, and rests in His forgiveness. When you blow it, God no longer requires you to purify yourself with rituals and sacrifices. This has been done through Christ. Now the message is to come confidently before His throne to find mercy and help when we are in need. The only one who can come confidently before His throne of grace is the one who trusts in the love of God given to us through Christ. The one who trusts in his or her own righteous abilities will avoid the throne because they are in fear. And the Bible says that the one who fears has not been made perfect in agape – God's love.

Grace teaches is to deny ungodliness by leading us out of the flesh. When you sin, stop groveling in defeat in the flesh. Look up to your Redeemer, rejoice in the hope of His mercies, and come boldly before His throne of grace.

True confession in the Christian's life is this. "I sinned and I need help to overcome. I confess my faith in Jesus, my Advocate." Then leave behind what is of the passing life of the flesh and pursue the future hope in the Spirit. No more needs to be done.

Seven times the word 'confession' is mentioned in the New Testament. One relates to receiving salvation by confessing Christ. Once was Pilate's confession that Jesus was blameless at His crucifixion. The rest relate to us confessing our faith in Him. We are told to hold fast to our confession of Christ.

When you sin, Satan will hurl condemnation and guilt at you. But you overcome by holding fast to the confession of your faith in Christ.

Stop giving credit to the devil. Stop giving power to sin. Stop trusting in condemnation. "Okay, Satan. I'll admit that you pulled one on me. I believed the lie of temptation and let you distract me. Now the truth has been revealed and your sham is finished. I'm out of here." That is as far as defeat should take us. The accuser will chase after us saying, "Look at your sin," but we must look at the Author and Finisher of our faith. All sin has already been defeated. Now it's time to stop wallowing among the dead.

I'm beating this point with repetitiveness because it is vital. I have never met a victorious Christian who tried to appease an angry God. I never experienced victory until I understood these things. Sin lost its grip when I began experiencing the promise of the Spirit. My sins once defeated me for days, weeks, and even months. There was a time in my life when I was so defeated by the flesh that I dropped out of church and abandoned the way of faith for more than three years.

There came a point when I said, "God I can't do this. I can't keep myself right. I can't live this Christian life."

It was as if God answered, "Well, now that you've finally figured that out, let's get started on the right way. Let's start trusting in grace and find out if these life-controlling sins can handle it."

You know what? They couldn't. The sins I could never defeat fell away without my effort. Do you know why? I was trying to use the flesh of human effort to defeat the sin of human weakness. I was empowering the flesh in the hopes that it could overcome itself.

It's not your role to defeat sin. It's not your role to overcome. Nor is it your role to produce spiritual maturity, bear fruit, produce righteousness, or fix other people. Consider **Galatians 5:16**

I say then: Walk in the Spirit, and you shall not fulfill the lust of the flesh.

It's the Holy Spirit's role to produce the things of the Spirit in your life. The more your life is filled with the grace of God, the more sin is driven out of your life. The flesh can't tolerate the Spirit, and sin has no place to set up its control. Sin has already been defeated, but the deeds of the sin remain in our body of flesh. Our choice is simple. Do we trust in the flesh, or do we trust in the Lord? The more I walk by faith in God, the more I learn how to become a receiver of grace. The more I look to the flesh, the greater I am tempted to sin, and the more I am tempted to trust in religion by human effort.

These things don't make sense to the human mind because they are only discerned through the Spirit. Until we walk by faith, we can never experience victory beyond what the flesh can produce.

When Jesus walked on the water and came to the disciples, they were in a fierce storm. They were rowing fruitlessly against the waves and wind. They were driven almost to despair. Jesus had been watching them rowing from a mountain near the lake. He waited for nearly nine hours before intervening. I believe he waited until they lost their strength and were losing ground to the wind. It would not be long before they would be either shipwrecked, or at best, driven back to where they began.

There journey began when Jesus said, "Get into the boat and go to the other side." It was a command God knew they didn't have the power to fulfill. They tried to obey and used every ounce of human effort to overcome the forces driving against them. When these men came to the end of themselves, Jesus stepped onto the stormy waters and walked toward the boat.

Peter was the first to recognize Him. As Jesus drew near, Peter said, "Lord, if it is really You, command that I come to you."

"Come," Jesus said, and Peter stepped into the miraculous. This mere man began walking on top of the waves as he pursued Jesus. But then temptation beckoned.

The tempter said, "Look at the waves." Peter took his eyes off of Jesus and saw high waves rushing toward him. "Look at that wind," the tempter said. "Isn't this the same wind that twelve of you couldn't row against?" Peter noticed the wind forcing his hair into his eyes and felt it pushing him off balance. He fell under its force, hit the water, and began to sink.

"Save me," he cried to Jesus.

Jesus reached into the sea and plucked Peter out. "Why did you doubt?" He asked. Jesus stepped into the boat, and the men looked up and saw that they were on the other side. Jesus took them to the destination He directed them to reach.

It was never in their power to reach the other side. It was Jesus who would take them. Like the law, the wind and waves served two main purposes. It revealed their weakness, and it revealed God's power. His strength was revealed in their weakness.

And that is what God wanted them to experience. They were partakers of God's mission. Many ships were moored on the opposite end of the sea. Only one dared tackle the storm, and it only did so because God called them to row against the storm.

It was never in Peter to walk on the waves. He was answering the call to come. God revealed Himself and invited Peter into the miracle of life in the Spirit. As long as Peter walked in the Spirit, the storms had no power. Because he was following Christ and trusting in His power, the sinking sea was a firm foundation. Or should I say that God created His firm foundation under Peter's feet. Once Peter trusted in temptation, the flesh became his strength and he didn't find the power to overcome.

Yet even in defeat, we see the message of grace. He sank and was powerless to overcome. Peter was drowning in the sea of temptation, and it was his own foolishness. All he had to do was to keep walking by faith. Faith got him out of the boat. Faith took him a few precious steps on top of the stormy waters. But once he returned his mind to the flesh, he cast away his faith in Christ. Jesus didn't leave him to the waves, but rescued him.

This is the message of grace. You can't overcome sin, even in your best strength. The church has been reduced to believing that if we can keep our head above water we are succeeding. And this is how most Christians live their lives. But God has given them the power to walk with Him in the Spirit where the storms, wind, and waves have no power. Those bobbing in the water are calling grace believers fools because it's impossible to walk on the water. "Get back in the boat," they are shouting.

Now it's for you to decide. Are you satisfied with the boat of religion? Is life only about rowing against the wind? Some step out on the waters, but then God plucks them from the sea of doubt. Religion points to them and says, "See. Grace doesn't work." Yet Jesus stands by our side. He continues to beckon us to trust in His power. Some step out while looking at their own feet for strength and fall. Some look to Christ and experience a moment of victory, and then fall to the distractions of either religion or temptation.

It's okay if you fall. God has your back. Just realize that you only fall when you take your eyes off Christ. Once we trust in anything other than the power of God, we are leaning on human strength.

Grace is the gift of the miraculous. It's nothing short of a miracle for a fleshly minded man or woman to enter into the life of the Spirit. Around you is the waves of resistance and the winds of temptation. Everything in this life is corrupted by sin and will try to knock you off your feet. Yet it has no power until you take your eyes off Christ. You will trust in what you are looking to.

Sin may have dominated you most of your life, but it has no power in the Spirit. Religion and religious, well-meaning people, may tempt you to trust in something other than the completed work of Christ. There will be times when you are persuaded to trust in temptation. Don't waste yourself trying to make God agree to rescue you. Hold to your confession, trust in His power to pluck you out of the water, and shake it off and go forward.

The high calling is, "Come." Only one disciple had the courage to answer that call. His faith gave him victory. His flesh fell. The flesh can do nothing other than fall into itself. Even if the flesh is trying to pursue Christ, it is incapable of walking in the Spirit of God's power. Only grace can establish you onto the firm foundation of God. A foundation that is not limited by circumstances. The troubled seas of life cannot prevent the foundation of God under your feet, but that foundation is only found in the Spirit.

If there is one thing grace has taught me is this: Failure is not my concern. Trust in Christ's victory and leave failure behind. The quicker you get out of the 'I've got to do something' mindset, the quicker you will put your eyes back on Christ. God is not burdened by your failures. He knows we are weak in faith, and sometimes our only focus is to receive faith from God so we can put faith in Him.

Have confidence in God's grace. You are already an overcomer in Christ, and this is to any who will trust in Him and rest their hope fully on His grace. Anything else is merely ashes in a passing life.

Go in grace and forget about the weaknesses of the flesh. Trust in God's victory given to us by grace. Enjoy the journey!

Find out more.

If you enjoyed this book, please rate it.

If you would like to know more about living by faith, you may enjoy these books by this author:

It is Finished! Step out of condemnation and into the completed work of Christ.

The Victorious Christian Life: Living in Grace and Walking in the Spirit.

The Promise of a Sound Mind : God's plan for emotional and mental health

God Loves the Addict: Experiencing Recovery on the Path of Grace

The Purpose of Grace

48542661R00071